THE ASIAN ANIMAL ZODIAC

THE ASIAN
ANIMAL ZODIAC

by Ruth Q. Sun

sketches by Norman Sun

CASTLE BOOKS

This edition published by arrangement with and permission of
Charles E. Tuttle Co., an imprint of Peri Plus Editions (Hong Kong)
with editorial offices at 153 Milk Street, Boston, MA 02109.

Published by Castle Books
a division of Book Sales, Inc.
114 Northfield Avenue
Edison, New Jersey 08837

Printed in the United States of America

ISBN 0-7858-1121-4

For my family Sun

Sun Pao-chen; Sun Tao Hsieh-hen; and,
of course,
Sun Nien-min (Norman), a scholar, a gentle man,
an artist, and a judge of fine wives

I've flown from my West
Like a desolate bird from a broken nest,
To learn thy secret of joy and rest.

—ERNEST FENOLLOSA

TABLE OF CONTENTS

ACKNOWLEDGMENTS

In preparing any book of this sort, one is always indebted deeply to many people for materials and for encouragement. Although I have done some rewriting in retelling these tales, they remain essentially as they have been known for many centuries in the lands of their origins. Concerning the special stories I have chosen to illustrate the twelve animals of the Asian animal zodiac (all traditional tales from Asian cultures), I am much in the debt of my present publisher, the Charles E. Tuttle Company of Tokyo, for permission to use from their collection of Korean folk legends, *The Story Bag* (Kim So-Un, ed.), the tale "A Dog Named Fireball."

From the Tuttle Company's *Japanese Children's Stories* (Florence Sakade, ed.), I have used, with their gracious permission, as well as that of the original translator of the tale, Meredith Weatherby, the ancient Japanese classic, "The Princess and the Herdboy."

From the book *Favorite Children's Stories of China and Tibet,* compiled by Lotta Carswell Hume and also published by the Tuttle Company, I have used, with permission, "How the Cock Got His Red Crown," "The Tower That Reached from Earth to Heaven," "How the Hare Bested the Wolf," and "How the Deer Lost His Tail."

Among well-known stories from the Japanese classics, I have used "Dojo-ji," a favorite of both the Noh and Kabuki theaters; "The White Hare of Inaba"; and "The Dragon Slayer." From the *Konjaku Monogatari* come the tales "A Monkey Returns a Kindness" (also retold by Hiroshi Naito in *Legends of Japan*, published by the Charles E. Tuttle Company) and "The Priest and the Monkey Deity."

For the following Korean stories, permission has been received from the London publishers Routledge and Kegan Paul, Ltd.: "The Deer and the Snake," "The Sheep Is Cousin to the Ox," and "The Rat's Bridegroom."

For all the charming animal stories from Vietnam included here, I owe a deep debt of gratitude to my former students at the University of Saigon, who helped me while away long and anxious hours by telling me some of the charming traditional tales of their beautiful land. These include "Why the Tiger Has Dark Stripes," "The Rabbit Bests the Tiger," "The Angel Who Became an Ox," "The Tale of the Tiger and the Mouse," "The Faithful Tiger," and "How the Horse Got His Lovely Big Teeth."

From the book *Chinese Fairy Tales and Folk Tales,* collected and translated by Wolfram Eberhard, I am indebted to the publishers (Kegan Paul, Trench, Trubner & Co., Ltd.) for permission to use, with some adaptation, the tales "The Rat and the Ox," "Whence Comes the Ox?" "Titsang P'usa and the Ox," and "Why Does the Cock Eat the Millipede?"

I am grateful also to the Gresham Publishing Company, Ltd., formerly of London, for the stories "The Yellow Dragon" and "The Dog Stone," from *Myths of China and Japan,* by Donald A. Mackenzie.

Finally, I am most grateful to my husband, Norman Sun, who translated from the Chinese classics, so that I might retell them in English, the stories "The Tailless Rat," "The Old Horse Knows the Way" (as originally written by Han Fei-tzu), "The Lamb Lost on a Branching Road," "The Monkeys and the Chestnuts" (as written by the great sage of the Confucian period, Chuang-tse), "How the Rooster Lost His Horns," "The Pig That Was Too Clever," "Dotting the Dragon's Eye," "The Guardian Snake," and "The Rabbit in the Moon."

For the lines quoted on the dedication page, I am indebted to the Harvard University Press, which gave its kind consent to my use of these lines from the longer poem "East and West" by Ernest Fenollosa, which was delivered as the Phi Beta Kappa poem at Harvard University in 1892.

The New York *Times* has given its consent to the

use of the round diagram called "The Cycle of Twelve," showing the relationship of the twelve zodiac animals to the basic *I Ching* designs, and centered by the symbolic *yin* and *yang* symbols.

From the Julian Press in New York City and Kelly & Walsh Ltd. in Shanghai I have received permission to use the chart, "The Cycle of Sixty," taken from the *Encyclopedia of Chinese Symbolism and Art Motives,* by C. A. S. Williams.

NOTE (*see facing page*): "The Ballad of the Hei Miao" refers to the Black Miao, a hill tribe of Chinese origin. This poem originally appeared in *Myths and Legends of China,* by E. T. C. Werner (London: George G. Harrap & Co.,1958), p. 406; it is reprinted by kind permission of the publishers. Although this primitive creation legend may originally have been part of the Black Miao's oral tradition, it was first translated, according to the publishers, by Mr. Werner.

THE BALLAD OF THE HEI MIAO
(from the Chinese)

Who made heaven and earth?
Who made insects?
Who made men?
Made male and female?
    I who speak don't know.

Heavenly king made heaven and earth
Ziene made insects,
Ziene made men and demons,
Made male and made female,
    How is it you don't know?

How made heaven and earth?
How made insects?
How made men and demons?
Made male and made female?
    I who speak don't know.

Heavenly king was intelligent,
Spat a lot of spittle into his hand,
Clapped his hands with a noise,
Produced heaven and earth,
Tall grass made insects,
Stories made men and demons,
Made male and made female.
    How is it you don't know?

INTRODUCTION

The origin of the Asian animal zodiac is lost somewhere in the mists of antiquity. It must have begun, certainly, in some remote past when the relationship of men to animals (and to all the wonders of nature) was close, warm, sympathetic. Probably it came about in an era when man still lived as a nomad, roaming at will among the mountains and valleys, utterly at peace with heaven and earth. It is for that reason, possibly, that the zodiac cycle is sometimes called the Yellow Road of the Sun, or the Zodiac of Hunters and Shepherds. And it is undoubtedly linked with a period in the life of primitive man when animistic religious beliefs included star and animal worship. It is known that the concept of sun worship was brought to the Far East from Mesopotamian countries, where the lion and the sun were associated in the zodiac. Egypt and Persia, too, had lion and sun cults.

The *I Ching* (Book of Changes), the most ancient of all Chinese records, shows a map of the heavens called *Ssu Fang*, with mythical animals having dominion not only over the Four Directions of the Universe, but also over the four seasons of the year. Winter and North were represented by the Black Tortoise (*Kuei She*); spring and the East by the Blue Dragon (*Ch'ing Lung*); summer and South by the Vermilion Bird, the Phoenix (*Chu Ch'ieh*); and autumn and West by the White Tiger (*Pai Hu*).

The rest of Asia probably took the zodiac of six wild and six domesticated animals from China, after its development and acceptance there. Certainly Chinese reference to it goes back very far indeed. The oracle bones of the Shang Period (1766– 1121 B.C.) show crude carvings of the horse, ox, sheep, pig, dog, tiger, and wild boar—all of them zodiac animals. There is also an ancient commentary which declares that the White Tiger is a metamorphosis of a star spirit called the "Star of Great Whiteness" (*T'ai Po Hsing*), believed to live in the Silver Stream of Heaven, the Milky Way—just as the Three-Legged Crow dwells in the sun and the White Hare in the moon.

There was some mention in literature of this method of reckoning as far back as the Han Dynasty (206 B.C.–A.D. 220), with the suggestion that Tartar mmigration during that period may have brought it to the Chinese. But the first explicit reference to the practice of marking years with the names of special animals comes from the T'ang Dynasty (A.D. 618–907), when it was recorded in one of the histories that an envoy of the Kirghis spoke of events as occurring in the Year of the Hare and the Year of the Horse. (A contrary school of thought holds that the twelve cyclical animals were borrowed from the Turks in the first century A.D.) It was probably later, during the Yuan (Mongol) Dynasty (A.D. 1277–1367) that use of the animal zodiac was popularized.

But despite the fact that the exact history of the system's development can never be established to everyone's satisfaction, every Asian knows under which animal sign he was born, and he usually gives his age by naming the animal year of his birth. He considers such knowledge essential to living, in fact, for all important decisions taken during his lifetime (especially the decision as to whom and when to marry) are affected by the individual's special animal, with its symbolism, and the whole astrological sphere into which it is tied. Indeed, the influence extends beyond life into the grave, for the animal zodiac is taken into consideration in determining where to bury the dead.

So inevitably the animal zodiac was caught up in legend. The tale that recounts the selection of the twelve special animals that make up the cycle (and the exclusion of others) relates that when Lord Buddha lay dying, he summoned all the animals of the forest to bid them farewell. These twelve—the rat, the ox (cow), the tiger, the rabbit, the dragon, the snake, the horse, the ram, the monkey, the rooster, the dog, and the pig (wild boar)—were the first to reach his bedside and so were honored by selection for this immortality in the order of their arrival.

Two tales account for the absence of the cat from the roster. One declares that when the call went forth for all the animals to gather round the dying Buddha, the cat was napping and couldn't be bothered to rouse herself to make the journey. The other states that the cat was forbidden a place among the mourners at the Buddha's deathbed because, in annoyance at its antics, the cat had killed the rat that Maya, the mother of Sakyamuni, had sent as medicine for her suffering son.

The cycle of twelve. © 1971 by the New York Times Co. Reprinted by permission.

The simple cycle of animal signs covering twelve years has been meshed into a longer cycle of sixty years (considered a man's normal life span) through a system of interrelationships, one with the Five Elements (positive and negative), the basic elements of creation: wood, fire, earth, metal, water. The entire concept is rooted in the ancient Chinese lunar calendar system which was used throughout the Far East until, in recent times, westerners introduced the more modern Roman solar calendar. Under the lunar system, the sixty-year cycle was arrived at by an interlocking arrangement of sets of characters, one of ten (the Ten Celestial Stems), and one of twelve (the Twelve Terrestrial Branches). These are combined in such a way that a complete cycle of sixty years is formed by a single revolution. The Chinese call this the Cycle of Cathay, and because of it a man's sixtieth birthday becomes a culminating event in life, marked by a special celebration called "The Return to the Beginning." When a repetition of the first combination becomes necessary, another cycle is started and continued in exactly the same manner as the first. In the western time system, ten decades form a century; for the Asians, five complete zodiac cycles are the exact equivalent of three centuries.

The whole system is thought to have been evolved by one Ta Nao around the twenty-seventh century B.C., and is described in the ancient *Book of Rites*. It is said that Ta Nao studied the properties of the Five Elements and calculated the revolving motion of certain constellations for the purpose of naming the days. By joining the first of the Ten Celestial Stem signs to the first of the Twelve Terrestrial Branch signs, the combination *Chia Tzu* is formed; and a succession of combinations continues until the tenth sign is reached, when a fresh start is begun, with the eleventh of the series of twelve branches being next attached to the sign *Chia*. The sixty combinations so formed are the Cycle of Sixty, and they are called *Chia Tzu*, or *Hua Chia Tzu*. During the Han Dynasty, this invention was made to apply to years as well as to months and days.

The cyclical signs play an enormously important role in Chinese divination, because of their supposed connection not only with the elements, or essences, but also with the *yin* and the *yang*, the positive and negative forces of the universe, and with the Eight Trigrams, which figuratively denote the evolution of nature and its cyclic changes. Asians recognize a close connection among geomancy, horoscopy, astronomy, and astrology—in fact, it is often difficult to tell where one ends and another begins. Climatic changes are thought to be produced by the moral conduct of the people through the agency of the sun, moon, and stars. In the computation of a favorable time to undertake any given enterprise, a happy combination of the eight horoscopic characters is arrived at—the eight characters being the four pairs of characters representing the year, month, day, and hour. By such means, the auspicious time for birth,

No. of year in Cycle	Name of year in Cycle (combined Stems and Branches)	Corresponding Elements		Symbolic Animals			74th	75th	76th	77th	78th
1	Chia Tzŭ 甲子	Mu 木	Wood	Shu 鼠	Rat		1744	1804	1864	1924	1984
2	I Chou 乙丑	" "	"	Niu 牛	Ox		1745	1805	1865	1925	1985
3	Ping Yin 丙寅	Ho 火	Fire	Hu 虎	Tiger		1746	1806	1866	1926	1986
4	Ting Mao 丁卯	" "	"	T'u 兎	Hare		1747	1807	1867	1927	1987
5	Wu Ch'ên 戊辰	T'u 土	Earth	Lung 龍	Dragon		1748	1808	1868	1928	1988
6	Chi Ssŭ 己巳	" "	"	Shê 蛇	Snake		1749	1809	1869	1929	1989
7	Kêng Wu 庚午	Chin 金	Metal	Ma 馬	Horse		1750	1810	1870	1930	1990
8	Hsin Wei 辛未	" "	"	Yang 羊	Ram		1751	1811	1871	1931	1991
9	Jên Shên 壬申	Shui 水	Water	Hou 猴	Monkey		1752	1812	1872	1932	1992
10	Kuei Yu 癸酉	" "	"	Chi 雞	Cock		1753	1813	1873	1933	1993
11	Chia Hsü 甲戌	Mu 木	Wood	Ch'üan 犬	Dog		1754	1814	1874	1934	1994
12	I Hai 乙亥	" "	"	Chu 猪	Boar		1755	1815	1875	1935	1995
13	Ping Tzŭ 丙子	Ho 火	Fire	Shu 鼠	Rat		1756	1816	1876	1936	1996
14	Ting Chou 丁丑	" "	"	Niu 牛	Ox		1757	1817	1877	1937	1997
15	Wu Yin 戊寅	T'u 土	Earth	Hu 虎	Tiger		1758	1818	1878	1938	1998
16	Chi Mao 己卯	" "	"	T'u 兎	Hare		1759	1819	1879	1939	1999
17	Kêng Ch'ên 庚辰	Chin 金	Metal	Lung 龍	Dragon		1760	1820	1880	1940	2000
18	Hsin Ssŭ 辛巳	" "	"	Shê 蛇	Snake		1761	1821	1881	1941	2001
19	Jên Wu 壬午	Shui 水	Water	Ma 馬	Horse		1762	1822	1882	1942	2002
20	Kuei Wei 癸未	" "	"	Yang 羊	Ram		1763	1823	1883	1943	2003
21	Chia Shên 甲申	Mu 木	Wood	Hou 猴	Monkey		1764	1824	1884	1944	2004
22	I Yu 乙酉	" "	"	Chi 雞	Cock		1765	1825	1885	1945	2005
23	Ping Hsü 丙戌	Ho 火	Fire	Ch'üan 犬	Dog		1766	1826	1886	1946	2006
24	Ting Hai 丁亥	" "	"	Chu 猪	Boar		1767	1827	1887	1947	2007
25	Wu Tzŭ 戊子	T'u 土	Earth	Shu 鼠	Rat		1768	1828	1888	1948	2008
26	Chi Chou 己丑	" "	"	Niu 牛	Ox		1769	1829	1889	1949	2009
27	Kêng Yin 庚寅	Chin 金	Metal	Hu 虎	Tiger		1770	1830	1890	1950	2010
28	Hsin Mao 辛卯	" "	"	T'u 兎	Hare		1771	1831	1891	1951	2011
29	Jên Shên 壬辰	Shui 水	Water	Lung 龍	Dragon		1772	1832	1892	1952	2012
30	Kuei Ssŭ 癸巳	" "	"	Shê 蛇	Snake		1773	1833	1893	1953	2013
31	Chia Wu 甲午	Mu 木	Wood	Ma 馬	Horse		1774	1834	1894	1954	2014
32	I Wei 乙未	" "	"	Yang 羊	Ram		1775	1835	1895	1955	2015
33	Ping Shên 丙申	Ho 火	Fire	Hou 猴	Monkey		1776	1836	1896	1956	2016
34	Ting Yu 丁酉	" "	"	Chi 雞	Cock		1777	1837	1897	1957	2017
35	Wu Hsü 戊戌	T'u 土	Earth	Ch'üan 犬	Dog		1778	1838	1898	1958	2018
36	Chi Hai 己亥	" "	"	Chu 猪	Boar		1779	1839	1899	1959	2019
37	Kêng Tzŭ 庚子	Chin 金	Metal	Shu 鼠	Rat		1780	1840	1900	1960	2020
38	Hsin Chou 辛丑	" "	"	Niu 牛	Ox		1781	1841	1901	1961	2021
39	Jên Yin 壬寅	Shui 水	Water	Hu 虎	Tiger		1782	1842	1902	1962	2022
40	Kuei Mao 癸卯	" "	"	T'u 兎	Hare		1783	1843	1903	1963	2023
41	Chia Ch'ên 甲辰	Mu 木	Wood	Lung 龍	Dragon		1784	1844	1904	1964	2024
42	I Ssŭ 乙巳	" "	"	Shê 蛇	Snake		1785	1845	1905	1965	2025
43	Ping Wu 丙午	Ho 火	Fire	Ma 馬	Horse		1786	1846	1906	1966	2026
44	Ting Wei 丁未	" "	"	Yang 羊	Ram		1787	1847	1907	1967	2027
45	Wu Shên 戊申	T'u 土	Earth	Hou 猴	Monkey		1788	1848	1908	1968	2028
46	Chi Yu 己酉	" "	"	Chi 雞	Cock		1789	1849	1909	1969	2029
47	Kêng Hsü 庚戌	Chin 金	Metal	Ch'üan 犬	Dog		1790	1850	1910	1970	2030
48	Hsin Hai 辛亥	" "	"	Chu 猪	Boar		1791	1851	1911	1971	2031
49	Jên Tzŭ 壬子	Shui 水	Water	Shu 鼠	Rat		1792	1852	1912	1972	2032
50	Kuei Chou 癸丑	" "	"	Niu 牛	Ox		1793	1853	1913	1973	2033
51	Chia Yin 甲寅	Mu 木	Wood	Hu 虎	Tiger		1794	1854	1914	1974	2034
52	I Mao 乙卯	" "	"	T'u 兎	Hare		1795	1855	1915	1975	2035
53	Ping Ch'ên 丙辰	Ho 火	Fire	Lung 龍	Dragon		1796	1856	1916	1976	2036
54	Ting Ssŭ 丁巳	" "	"	Shê 蛇	Snake		1697	1857	1917	1977	2037
55	Wu Wu 戊午	T'u 土	Earth	Ma 馬	Horse		1798	1858	1918	1978	2038
56	Chi Wei 己未	" "	"	Yang 羊	Ram		1799	1859	1919	1979	2039
57	Kêng Shên 庚申	Chin 金	Metal	Hou 猴	Monkey		1800	1860	1920	1980	2040
58	Hsin Yu 辛酉	" "	"	Chi 雞	Cock		1801	1861	1921	1981	2041
59	Jên Hsü 壬戌	Shui 水	Water	Ch'üan 犬	Dog		1802	1862	1922	1982	2042
60	Kuei Hai 癸亥	" "	"	Chu 猪	Boar		1803	1863	1923	1983	2043

The cycle of sixty: five complete cycles or 300 years (A.D. 1744–2043).

marriage, death, housebuilding, journeys, and all kinds of human activities can be worked out.

In the matter of marriage, the natural elements play an important role. For example, men born under the sign of the wood element should preferably wed women born under the fire element. Their next best choice would be a woman born under the element of water. They should avoid contracting a marriage with someone born under the sign of the metal element. While they could get along all right with a mate born under the earth element, this would not prove an ideal match.

In the same way, men of the fire element should strive to wed women of the earth element. Their second choices should be women of the wood element. They may succeed in living happily ever after with women of metal, but women of the water element are definitely to be shunned.

Men of the earth element should marry metal or fire women, avoid wood women, but may succeed with water women.

Metal men do best with water women, next best with earth women. They should avoid fire women, but will find a wood woman only half bad.

Men of the water element should marry wood women, will find metal women next best, can manage to get along with fire women, but must, at all cost, avoid earth women. Marriage with mates born under the same element (wood man and wood woman, fire man and fire woman, earth man and earth woman) is always to be avoided.

The Five Elements are also helpful as guides to selection of a useful and appropriate occupation. In brief, those born under the wood element are advised to select work connected in some way with water or fire; those born under the element of fire should work in some way with earth or wood; earth element people, with fire or metal; water element people, with wood or metal.

All of this becomes increasingly complicated and esoteric. But the twelve animals of the Yellow Road of the Sun remain forever simple and comprehensible, with their all-too-human characteristics. Certain combinations of animals are declared to be mutually antipathetic. For example, the rat hates the sheep's horns, and is also an enemy of the snake; the tiger despises the short bill of the cock; the rabbit simply cannot endure the monkey's constant playfulness and practical jokes; the dragon dislikes the pig's black face; and the ox abominates the laziness of the horse, which will not help him to plough.

Perhaps these very human characteristics explain why the animals continue to play such an important and charming part in the myth and legendry of Asian culture. And so I hope that this animal lore, these animal tales from various Asian lands, may reveal some of this charm and timelessness to the western reader.

—Ruth Sun

1 THE RAT

TZU   SHU

The Rat

Although despised in the West, the rat has traditionally been a highly respected rodent in the Orient. The Chinese thought highly enough of him, in fact, to give him first place in their animal zodiac, where he is declared to represent the beginning of things, or the first cause. According to a popular Buddhist legend, however, the rat earned his lead-off position in the zodiac through typical craftiness and guile. The story goes that when Lord Buddha lay dying, he summoned all the animals to his bedside to say farewell. The faithful ox got a head start and was leading the lengthy procession when the rat, scampering along, caught up to him and begged for a ride on his back. The patient, good-natured ox agreed to this. But when they reached the entrance to the pavilion where Lord Buddha lay, the rat suddenly leaped from the back of the ox and raced inside ahead of him, thereby becoming the first arrival at the bedside. As a reward for such respect, the Buddha honored the rat with the first position in the zodiac.

Despite his universal reputation for trickery and stealth, Asians have always tended to respect the rat for the intelligence he displays in locating, acquiring, and hoarding his booty. In this way, the rat has become a symbol of industry and prosperity. In fact, the rat's presence in a home or barn has been considered auspicious, a symbol of prosperity, since the rat will remain only where there is food. Indeed, the Japanese have a proverb: "Getting rich means to invite the rat!"

The sole Chinese reservation about the rat seems to be that children born in the Year of the Rat will not become good scholars (perhaps because they will be too busy making money). The Chinese also think that the rat shows impartiality: he is good to businessmen in making money, but also good to thieves, robbers, and others of that ilk. So there may be an increase in crime in the rat's year!

In Asian mythology and art, the rat is often shown as one of the attendants of Daikoku, the god of wealth, one of the popular Seven Gods of Happiness. The name "Daikoku" means "Big Black One," and so this god is often shown with a dark face; however, he is more usually pictured as a smiling old man, looking more benevolent than rich old men often do, and holding his magic mallet and a bale of rice at which rats are nibbling. Daikoku is sometimes thought to have had his birthplace in India, where his counterpart is called Mahakala (meaning "Big Black One"), a god of vegetation. It has also been declared that Daikoku was originally a Japanese Shinto deity, Okuninushi, the Master of the Great Land, who was assimilated with the Indian deity and taken over by the Buddhists. The rat serves Daikoku as a companion and a messenger, even though Daikoku must guard his accumulation of stored rice from the rat's depredations. The rat's powers of rapid multiplication also imply the rapid multiplication of riches. Daikoku's festival day is held annually on the "day of the rat."

The rat appears in numerous Asian legends. One tells of the jealousy of the Buddhist statues in a temple when they saw the people bringing their offerings to Daikoku and praying to him for prosperity in life. Because this was against their interests, the Buddhist statues asked the guardian of hell, Emma O, to get rid of Daikoku. Emma O, in an agreeable mood, dispatched a prominent devil named Shiro to earth to take care of the matter. Discovering Daikoku in his rice godowns admiring his treasure, Shiro hid himself to await the propitious moment for attack. But alert Daikoku had heard footsteps, so he sent his chief rat attendant to investigate. The rat discovered Shiro, chased him outside, and attacked him with a prickly holly branch, eventually chasing him back to the portals of hell.

(Since then, the holly has been a talisman against evil. In the West, use of decorative Christmas holly started as insurance against evil.)

One favorite Japanese legend about the rat concerns a childhood incident in the life of the famous painter Sesshu. One day, in punishment for having wasted his time, the boy was tied by his teacher to an outdoor post. To while away the time, young Sesshu drew pictures of rats in the sand with his toe. So lifelike were these rodents that they came to life, in fact, and gnawed away the ropes that bound the young artist, freeing him.

Other legends concern spirits of the dead that frequently return to earth in the guise of rats to assist a friend in need or to confound an enemy. One such tale is about a historic character named Raigo who, disillusioned by a broken imperial pledge, became a priest, went on a hunger strike in the monastery, and died. His unappeased soul then terrorized the imperial palace in the form of thousands of rats.

In both China and Japan, small carved ivory figures of the rat may be given as good luck gifts, or as amulets to ward off bad luck and ensure prosperity.

There is an ancient tradition that a house is safe so long as rats live in it, since they have a way of knowing beforehand of the coming of flood or fire, and will disappear before disaster strikes. The presence of the rat is therefore thought of in many places as assurance of the safety of the home.

The Year of the Rat is considered a time of hard work and constant activity, but one that will assure abundant food for everyone. It is a year for steady gain, a little at a time, after the fashion of the rat, who is never idle, who is always seeking food, but who transports it a little at a time over the course of the day, never in large bulk. The food of the rat is accumulated by dint of constant labor. The Rat Year also stands for timidity and humbleness, a year in which everyone works steadily and patiently but remains humble about success. Because of the rat's proclivity for rapid multiplication of its species, his year also anticipates quick expansion in every field of human activity.

People born in the Year of the Rat therefore exhibit these same qualities. They are active, hardworking, their lives marked by constant effort and steady accumulation, a little at a time, rather than by large strokes of fortune. They are patient, alert, persevering, and marked by deep humility. They may lean to the stingy side, with a tendency to pinch pennies, but they save and scrimp and work hard for the things they really want. And to those whom they really love, they are generous, even to the point of squandering their hard-won wealth.

In general, such people are quite charming in their personalities. They keep themselves in check, although underneath they are capable of a deep, though controlled, anger. They are honest, ambitious, restrained, persistent, given to self-denial, and prone to gossip.

An individual born in the Year of the Rat is best married to someone from the years of the dragon, the monkey, or the ox, since such people will be best suited to them temperamentally. Second choice would fall upon someone from the years of the rat, the tiger, the snake, the dog, or the wild boar. The worst possible choice of mate would be someone born in the Year of the Horse—especially someone born in the Year of the Fiery Horse (which comes only once in every sixty years). A man marrying a woman born in that inauspicious (for females) year will be certain to die before his time!

The rat's bridegroom

Once upon a time there lived a family of rats. When the eldest daughter of the family grew up and became of marriageable age, her parents decided that they must find the most powerful person in the world and ask him to become her husband. They felt that such a beautiful and well-mannered and poised daughter as theirs deserved nothing less than the most eligible bachelor in all the world.

So one day the parents got dressed up nicely, combed and washed and at their neatest, and they went to call upon the Sun. "Good day, Mr. Sun," said they. "Our eldest daughter has grown up and it is now time that she was happily married. So we are seeking the most powerful person in all the world to be her bridegroom. Judging from your high position and great effect, you seem to be the most powerful of all. And so we have come here today to invite you to be her husband."

But the Sun shook his head, and then said with a smile: "It may appear to you that I am the most powerful person in the world, but actually this is not so. Mr. Cloud is more powerful than I am, for he can cover my face and keep me from shining. So I recommend Mr. Cloud to you."

Mr. and Mrs. Rat thought over what the Sun had told them, and they concurred that Mr. Cloud must indeed be the most powerful of all. So they called on him and said: "Good day, Mr. Cloud. Our daughter has grown up, and now it is time she was married. We wish to invite the most powerful person in the world to be her husband, and so we are now here to welcome you as her bridegroom, for you can even cover the face of the Sun to keep him from shining."

But Mr. Cloud shook his head. "Yes, I can cover the face of the sun and keep him from shining," he said. "Yet in spite of that, I am not the most powerful, for Mr. Wind blows me away with one fat puff, whether I wish to go or not. He is far more powerful than I, and so I recommend him to you for your purpose."

Mr. and Mrs. Rat thought the whole matter over with careful consideration. They decided, in the end, that Mr. Wind must indeed be more powerful than Mr. Cloud. So they went to Mr. Wind in his cave and said: "Good day, Mr. Wind. Our daughter is now grown up, and we feel that the time has come for her to marry. We want to invite the most powerful person in the world to be her bridegroom, and so we have come here to welcome you as her husband, for your power is clear. You can blow Mr. Cloud away, whether he wishes to go or not!"

But Mr. Wind shook his fat cheeks and laughed. "I do appreciate your kind offer," said he. "It's certainly true that I am quite powerful, but I must in honesty tell you that there is one more powerful than I. And I mean the stone Buddha in Unzin, in the Province of Zolla. His feet are planted so firmly on the ground that, blow as I will, I cannot budge him in the slightest. He has a halo on his head, but I cannot even blow that off! He is surely the most powerful of all, so I recommend him strongly to you."

So Mr. and Mrs. Rat trudged off and called upon the

Stone Buddha of Unzin. Mrs. Rat spoke up for the family: "Our daughter is now old enough to wed, and we are pleased to invite you to be her bridegroom, since you are the most powerful of all."

The stone Buddha smiled, and answered them in a slow and gentle voice: "I do thank you for this kind offer. But there is one yet more powerful than I. He is the young rat who lives beneath my feet. One day he will undermine me completely, and I will fall. Mrs. Rat, I am truly at the mercy of the rats!"

Mr. and Mrs. Rat were pleased, for they realized at last that the only suitable bridegroom for their lovely daughter was a young rat. So they returned home happily, and on a crisp fall day they married their eldest daughter off to a fine, serious young rat who was already giving evidence of reliability and integrity in rat affairs.

*   *   *

"The Rat's Bridegroom" is a Korean fable. Undoubtedly the Koreans—especially country folk, like their counterparts all over the world—are very familiar with the rat and his depredations, and it is natural that tales about him entered their folklore.

The tailless rat

Once upon a time there was a rat who could never make

up his mind about anything. He was totally indecisive, poor thing! No matter what you asked him, he could never produce a flat, definite answer to your question.

For example, if you said to him: "Isn't today a fine day?" he would ponder a bit and then answer you: "Welllll . . . yes . . . today is pretty fine . . . but then, maybe it *isn't* quite so fine. To tell the truth, I don't know whether this kind of weather is good or bad!"

If you asked him: "Do you have time to go shopping with me this afternoon?" he might say: "Oh, I'm sorry! I don't have time in the afternoon. In the morning I might have some time . . . but no, no, no, I think I'm going to be quite busy in the morning, after all. Maybe in the afternoon I'll be freer . . . but . . . but . . . it seems as if it may rain in the afternoon. Why don't we wait until after lunch to make up our minds? Anyhow, this is no urgent matter; we don't have to come to a decision right away, do we? Why should we hurry?"

Sometimes people would say to him: "Mr. Rat, how many sons and daughters do you have?" In such a situation, he would reply:

"Oh, well now . . . I think I have seven sons and eight daughters . . . or, let me see now . . . perhaps seven daughters and eight sons . . . oh well, anyway, I am sure I have more than ten children . . . or perhaps now it's somewhere between twenty and thirty. Yes indeed, in any case I'd guess I have at least twenty. I'm pretty sure I do. I'm quite certain about that. . . ."

One time a big storm arose about midnight. It appeared that it might totally destroy Mr. Rat's home. All those in the house with him were awakened by the storm's howling, and they cried out:

"Oh dear, let's run away from this storm! Don't sleep

anymore! Get up, everybody, we must run for our lives!"

But Mr. Rat, half awake and half asleep, replied drowsily:

"It's still dark outside. Why should we get up so early? I . . . ah . . . why it seems as if it must be raining outside, is that right? Oh yes indeed, it *is* raining, isn't it?"

The other rats kept on calling:

"Hurry, hurry! Don't delay a moment! Let's get away from here before our house blows down and we are killed!"

Then they added:

"If you're not going to come along, we'll just go ahead by ourselves anyway." So away they scampered to safety.

Mr. Rat said to himself: "Did they say this house might fall down? Why, this house is in excellent condition! It won't fall down. We've lived here for a very long time, and the house has *never* fallen down. No indeed, never!"

While he was uttering these very words to himself, the wind was getting stronger and stronger, and the rain was coming down harder and harder. Still this uncertain rat couldn't make up his mind to stay or go.

After some second and third, and even some fourth, thoughts, he said:

"*Ai-ya*! The house *is* shaking rather badly! Maybe it will really tumble down after all! Well, perhaps then I should leave too."

But as soon as he got to the door, he looked outside and cried:

"Oh, my goodness, this rain is so heavy! I'd better not go out into it!"

While he was uttering these words, the entire house suddenly collapsed about him.

"*Tse, tse, tse, tse, tse,*" squealed the rat.

Was the rat killed? No, he couldn't even be decisive enough to be killed outright. When the house fell down upon him, his body was already outside the door. So the house collapsed not on him, exactly, but on his tail, which was still inside the house, in the front hall. A falling beam severed the tail quite neatly.

So ever after that, this poor soul was a tailless rat! But the loss of his tail changed his personality about, so that he finally became quite decisive. No longer did he waver in making up his mind. He made all his commitments quickly and firmly. Thus finally he won the respect of all the other rats, and of his many friends.

* * *

"The Tailless Rat" is an old Chinese folk tale.

 # The rat and the ox

There was once a half-god living among men—it is hard to say just when—who wanted to find twelve animals for the zodiac, in order to name the years. He had already placed the dragon, the snake, the tiger, and the hare, when the rat and the ox began to quarrel about which was the bigger. Naturally the body and the appearance of the ox was much larger, and when he heard the claim of the rat, he shook his horns and shouted out: "Everyone knows that I, the ox, am big and immeasurably strong. How can a rat that weighs only a few pounds dare to compete with me? I call it ridiculous!"

The sly, cunning rat merely laughed coldly at the boasts of the ox, and said: "Everyone is conceited about his own size and capabilities. That is no criterion. We must submit the question to the will of the majority. It is quite true that I am only a poor little rat, but I will measure myself with you today."

Fearing that the battle of words between the ox and the rat would develop into a serious quarrel, the half-god quickly interrupted:

"Naturally a rat is not so big as an ox. But, since the rat won't accept that fact, we must entrust the matter to the decision of the crowd. That is assuredly the just way to decide. I suggest that you think the matter over, and then go outside to hear the people's verdict." The ox agreed at once to this suggestion of the half-god, for he thought that his victory was assured.

The rat pretended to be in despair, however, and lay on a chair sunk in gloom and depression. "Of course we can go on and on about this," he thought, "but I must be at least a little bigger before I can appear before the people."

Seeing the rat so disheartened, the ox thought that, whatever happened, the rat would be much smaller than he was; and so, when the rat suggested that he be given time to at least double his size, the ox readily agreed. He himself was not one whit disturbed because he was still at least one hundred times larger than that rat.

Meantime the rat was gobbling down a two-pound piece of cheese he had found, and he washed that down with a quart of milk, after overturning the bottle. He also found some meat and vegetable snacks here and there, and in less time than you might suppose, Mr. Rat had grown to twice his previous size and weight. At that point, the ox and the rat went out together into the town.

"Look there!" exclaimed the people. "Never before have we seen such a huge rat! My, he really is an incredibly big fellow. Strapping!" From the moment they left the house until their return to it after walking up and down and all about the town, the ox and the rat heard on all sides only exclamations of wonder at the size of the rat. But no one even bothered to look twice at the ox, because people see huge, lumbering oxen every single day, whereas no one had ever before seen quite so huge a rat.

The good-natured but stupid ox had fallen into the rat's trap, but he never even realized that he had been tricked! He thought only that the people's eyes must be failing. Since he lost the contest, he had practically no dignity left. He lost face completely. And from that time forward, the rat was acknowledged the first animal in the zodiac.

*   *   *

"The Rat and the Ox" is my version of an often-told Chinese folktale.

2 THE OX

丑 牛

CH'OU   NIU

The Ox

The water buffalo, the species of ox best known in the Orient, is a favorite theme in art and legend in that part of the world. In almost any typical rural scene, from the Yangtze valley south, both in China and indeed in all of Southeast Asia, this gentle, patient draft animal is seen turning the water wheels and ploughing up the mud of the rice fields preparatory to planting. He is usually attended by either a small boy or an old man, who is frequently perched on the animal's rump. The venerable sage Lao Tzu is often depicted in art riding on a buffalo. Another favorite theme is the small boy, perched precariously near the animal's tail, playing on a bamboo flute.

The ox goes far back in Asian history. As early as the Shang and Chou Dynasties in China, a favorite decoration on bronzes was the head of such a bovine creature, with wide, flat horns sloping sharply backwards. Remains of such an ox-like creature, possibly an extinct form of water buffalo, have been found in excavations at Anyang in Honan Province, dating from the Shang-Yin Period.

Only because of the sly trick played upon him by

the rat is the ox the second in order in the animal zodiac. Outwitted though he was, the slow-moving, patient beast never complained. Although famous for his gentleness, this animal nonetheless possesses hidden reservoirs of great strength. If he is really irritated or enraged, he can run as fast as a bull and become quite ferocious. But such a thing would occur only in a rare and unusual situation. Throughout most of Asia, the water buffalo is used as a beast of burden to perform most of the tasks done by the horse in the West.

The ox appears in many Asian legends. One Japanese tale tells of an old woman in the provinces, so selfish and greedy that she kept herself too busy to visit the temple, even on festival days. One year, on the eighth day of the fourth month (Buddha's birthday), when she was washing cloth at a stream, an ox passing by caught a piece of the old lady's cloth on its horns. The old woman, determined to get her cloth back, ran after the animal until he disappeared within the grounds of the Zenkoji temple. The old woman stopped briefly to worship the temple's Kannon image, and miraculously, from that moment on, she became a pious woman. As if that in itself weren't enough, the mountain behind the temple became marked by a white band similar to the lost piece of cloth. People began to call the mountain Mt. Nunobiki (cloth-pulling).

Oddly enough, the ox has been used in the practice of sorcery and magic. A woman who visits an isolated shrine at the Hour of the Ox (very late at night) and takes part in a prescribed ritual can punish an unfaithful lover or get even with a rival.

There is only one example of the use of bullocks in warfare, however. Japanese history relates that during the Genji-Heike wars of the twelfth century, one of Yoritomo's generals, Yoshinaka, won an important victory at the battle of Kurikara by tying blazing torches to the horns of a herd of bullocks and driving them into the enemy ranks. The terrified cattle stampeded, forcing the foe backward to certain death over a steep mountain precipice.

All over the world the bullock has been the traditional symbol of spring and agriculture because of his association with the plough and with springtime festivals, including those of ancient Greece and India. Bull gods have, in fact, been prominent in all religions from earliest recorded times. To the Minotaur of Crete the ancient Greeks sent, every nine years, a sacrificial tribute of seven youths and seven maidens. The Babylonians worshipped the bull god Baal; the Egyptians, Apis; the Phoenicians, Moloch; the Assyrians, winged, human-headed bulls; the Syrians, Attis; the Hittites, Sadan. In India, the sacred white bull is the mount of the third god of the Hindu triad, Siva the Destroyer, who himself personifies the bull's characteristics: the eternal reproductive power of nature, perpetually recreating itself after disintegration. From this has stemmed the practice in that country of considering cattle sacred, and protecting them.

In China the word *niu*, which means cattle, is thought to represent the sound the animal makes, just as the character, or ideograph, for *niu* (牛), in its original form, pictured the animal.

In Japan the ox is often associated with the peach

tree and is used as a symbol by the Zen Buddhist sect. Also in Japan, the ox is closely associated with the great *Bon* festival, the festival of lanterns in midsummer, when the spirits of deceased ancestors return for their annual visit to the family. They are supposed to ride back on a bullock, so, in order to accommodate them, a toy animal made of a small eggplant propped on four stick legs is placed at a short distance from the house, so that the spirit may clamber aboard and complete its journey in style.

The Year of the Ox is generally considered a good year, one in which difficulties can be overcome by steady, patient effort backed by strength. Slow, sure progress is the rule for the Year of the Ox—not impulsive, thoughtless action. According to Asian astrology, people born in the Year of the Ox possess the characteristics of that animal. They appear outwardly deliberate and slow-moving, but they may be goaded into irritation and acts of rage. Although they may sometimes seem to be indecisive and slow to come to a decision, they are really patient and persevering. When they set their minds on something, they usually won't give up until they attain their goal. Their steady, consistent effort brings them ultimate success. Ox-year people are really alert, but just not given to talking much; they are patient, however, and can inspire confidence in others.

Such people are extremely dextrous and can do almost anything with their hands. Though placid and easygoing on the surface, they are remarkably stubborn and hate to fail at anything they have undertaken. If they are opposed, they can become quite unpleasant. They are reserved in their emotions, never demonstrative.

Ox-year people should avoid marriage with anyone born in the year of the ram, and also with people of the horse or dog years. They will find their best mates among those born in the snake, cock, or rat years. The second-best choice of life partner would come from among those born in the ox, dragon, rabbit, monkey, or wild boar years.

 # The angel who became an ox

At the time the planet Earth was created, the land was barren. There were no trees, no plants, no vegetation of any kind. The landscape was empty, dull, gray, monotonous. And human beings, sad to say, had no cereals or grains of any kind to eat.

The Jade Emperor, who reigned in Heaven, wanted to spare mankind the horrid fate of dying from starvation. He also wanted to make the Earth look more beautiful. So he thought about this for quite some time, and finally he devised a plan. He then summoned all his angels to his palace. Looking directly at then, he said:

"Who among you is willing to help me bring joy and happiness to men on the Earth, men now in distress?"

One of the angels, named Kim Quang, instantly

volunteered his services and, with great interest, offered to take charge of carrying out the will of the Jade Emperor.

Whereupon the Jade Emperor gave Kim Quang two heavy loads in baskets on a shoulder pole. One basket was filled with rice paddy, the other with grass seed. The god recommended that Kim Quang first sow the rice paddy over the earth, leaving the grass seed for any plots of field left over when the paddy was used up.

"If you do exactly as I say, I shall reward you," declared the Jade Emperor. "But if you disobey me in any way, I shall certainly punish you."

Quickly agreeing to the conditions laid down, Kim Quang prepared to set off for Earth with his shoulder-pole baskets of paddy and seed.

But alas! Kim Quang was an absent-minded angel. When he reached Earth, he scattered the grass seed first over all the land. And everywhere that it was sowed, the grass grew rapidly and luxuriantly. By the time the absent-minded angel remembered the instruction of the Jade Emperor correctly, it was too late to mend the error, for there was only a small area of the Earth left where the rice was free to grow.

Learning what had happened on Earth, the Jade Emperor was enraged with his uncooperative angel. Using his magic power, the emperor transformed Kim Quang into a buffalo, so that he could browse on the growing grass. He promised that whenever the buffalo could cut all the grass clean down to the bare ground, he could be changed back into his angelic form.

But never came that day!

*   *   *

This story is a favorite tale in Vietnamese legendry, and was told to me by my students at the University of Saigon. Since Vietnamese culture is heavily indebted to the Chinese, it may originally have been a Chinese tale.

 Whence comes the ox?

In ancient times, man had a hard life and was never able to get enough to eat. Sometimes he ate every third day, sometimes only every fifth or sixth day, and he was always hungry, although he worked day and night. Really, he was to be pitied.

The Heavenly Emperor was sorry for men, who ceaselessly labored without getting enough to eat, and so he ordered his subject the ox (that is, the Ox Star in the sky) to go down to Earth and say to the people: "If you men are energetic enough, you can have one meal every three days regularly."

But the ox misunderstood his orders. He went quickly down to Earth and announced to the people: "The Heavenly Emperor says you shall have three meals a day and not starve anymore."

When he then returned to Heaven to make his report, the Heavenly Emperor punished the Ox Star for his error by sending him back to Earth to assist men with their ploughing.

"I told you to tell men," said the Heavenly Emperor, "that they should have one meal every three days, but

you have now promised them three meals every day!
Just think of it—men have only two hands and two feet
apiece. How can they ever prepare three meals a day?
It is all your fault, and you must answer for it! You must
go down to Earth and help men plough, so that they
can really get these three meals a day you have promised
them in my name."

The ox therefore went down to Earth permanently,
no longer a star, but a large, strong animal, and he
helped men to plough the ground. The oxen now on
Earth all came originally straight from Heaven. Perhaps
that is why they are quiet and patient.

*　　　*　　　*

"Whence Comes the Ox?" is one version of a Chinese myth.

 ## Titsang P'usa and the ox

In former times there were no oxen on Earth; man had
to plough the fields with his own power, and that was
very tiring indeed. The kindhearted Titsang P'usa was
sorry for them, so one day he said to Yu Huang-ti:
"Mankind has such a hard time of it, tilling the fields.
Couldn't we send down the strong ox from Heaven to
help with the ploughing?"

Yu Huang-ti considered this for a moment, and then
he replied:

"No! Men on Earth are not kindhearted. So long as the ox remains young and strong, with a stout back, and can help with the work, man will treat him well. But when the ox becomes worn out in service, and too weak to plough any more, then men will turn against him, kill him, eat his flesh, and wear his hide."

But Titsang P'usa broke in, saying: "Men are not really so bad as all that. Let me be the guarantor for them. If they kill the ox, eat his flesh, and strip off his skin, I will go down to Hell myself."

Because he saw how earnest Titsang P'usa was, Yu Huang-ti granted his request.

Down to Earth to help with the ploughing came the ox. And at first (as might be expected) man treated him very well, because this wonderful animal was so strong, yet so gentle and patient, and could plough so well. But the moment he became old and helpless, men slaughtered him, ate his flesh, skinned him, and used the hide to make clothing—all this despite the fact that the poor ox wept bitter tears before his death and begged for mercy. Men paid absolutely no heed to his prayers.

Yu Huang-ti was so enraged by this fact that he did indeed banish Titsang P'usa to Hell, where, in punishment, he was made to keep his eyes perpetually closed, except on the thirtieth day of the seventh month. That is Titsang P'usa's day, and on it men on Earth light incense in honor of the saint who tried to be a benefactor of the animals.

*   *   *

The myth "Titsang P'usa and the Ox," which so cleverly reveals the cruelty of men to animals, even to those which are their benefactors, has its origin in ancient China.

The princess and the herdboy

This is a tale of long and long ago, when the king of the sky was still busily making stars to hang in the heavens at night. The king had a very beautiful daughter. She was called the Weaving Princess, because she sat at her loom all day long every day of the world. She wove the most delicate stuff that can be imagined, as delicate as a dream. It was so light and airy, so thin and smooth, that it was hung among the stars in the sky and draped down toward the earth. In fact, it was the cloth that we now call clouds and fog and mist.

The king of the sky was very proud of his daughter because she could weave so skillfully and was such a help to him. Making the sky was a big job and kept him very busy indeed, so he needed all the help he could possibly get. But still, one day he looked up from his tasks and he noticed that the Weaving Princess was becoming pale.

"Well now, young lady," said the king to his daughter, "you've been working too hard, I fear. So tomorrow you must take a holiday. Go out and play among the stars all day. After that you can help me. I still need much more mist and fog, and many more clouds."

The princess was very happy to be given a holiday, as anyone can imagine. She'd always wanted to go wading in the stream called the Milky Way that flowed right through the center of the sky. But never before had she found the time to do that.

So she put on her prettiest frock and ran out among the stars, right over to the Milky Way. And there, in the middle of the stream, she saw a handsome boy, washing a cow in the water.

"Hello," said the boy to the princess. "Who are you?"

"I'm really the star Vega," she answered him. "But everyone calls me Weaving Princess."

"I'm the star Altair," said the boy. "But everyone calls me Herdboy because I tend the cows that belong to the king of the sky. Won't you come over to my house and see where I live?"

So, when the princess agreed to that, the herdboy helped her up to the cow's back and led her across the stream. They had a wonderful time together all day long, the princess and the herdboy, and were so contented in each other's company that the princess forgot all about returning home to help her father!

When she failed to show up, the king of the sky became very anxious. He dispatched a magpie as his messenger to find the princess and tell her to return home at once. But when the magpie spoke to the princess, she was having such a fine time with her new friend that she refused to listen. Finally the king had to go himself to fetch her home.

"You've been quite bad, you know," said the king to his daughter. "Just look at the sky—not even finished yet. You've stayed away thinking only of your own pleasures. But the sky still needs clouds and mists and fog. So you can never have another holiday! What do you think of that? You'll just have to stay here and weave all the time."

Then the king poured more and more star water into the Milky Way. Until now it had been a shallow stream that you could wade across, but the king poured in so much star water that it became a deep, deep river. Now the princess and the herdboy lived on opposite sides of an impassable stream, and there was no way at all that they could get across to see each other again.

So the princess went into her little house in the sky and sat unhappily before her loom. She had fallen in love with the herdboy, and she was so lonely and longed for him so much that she couldn't weave at all. Instead, she just sat there weeping all the time. And the sky became emptier and emptier, with no clouds, no mist, no fog.

Finally the king said: "Please, my little princess, you mustn't cry all the time. I really need your clouds and mists and fog for my sky. So let me make a bargain with you. If you'll go to work and weave again, and work hard at it, I'll let you go spend one day each year with Herdboy."

When she heard that, the princess was happy again, so happy that she went right to work, and she has been working hard ever since.

And once each year, on the seventh night of the seventh moon, the king of the sky keeps his promise to Weaving Princess. He sends a flock of magpies to the Milky Way, and, with their extended wings touching, they make a bridge across the deep river. Then the princess runs quickly across the bridge of magpies to where Herdboy is waiting for her. And for one whole day and one whole night the young lovers can be together again!

And the Japanese and the Chinese celebrate that day and evening as a holiday. The Japanese call it Tanabata-Sama (The Seventh Night of the Seventh Month). They hope very much that it won't rain then, because if it does, then the lovers must wait another full year for their reunion. But if it is fair weather, then they notice that on that day and evening no magpies at all are to be seen. They have all flown to the skies to make the bridge so that the princess and the herdboy can be together again. And earth people rejoice with them by decorating bamboo branches with bright pieces of paper and waving them at the sky, to remind the king of the sky of his promise, as well as to thank him for keeping it.

And if you look closely, you can see the bright stars Vega and Altair in conjunction on that night!

*   *   *

The ancient legend called "The Princess and the Herdboy" is a common tale all through Asia because the conjunction of the stars that it personalizes is a favorite holiday each July 7. It is especially well-liked in Japan, and the story as it appears here is adapted from the version translated by Meredith Weatherby from the Japanese.

3 THE TIGER

YIN   HU

The Tiger

 The tiger, together with the dragon, holds the most honorable and ancient place in Oriental lore. Indeed, these two represent the two supreme animal powers: the tiger with dominion over the earth, and the dragon with dominion over the sky. The earliest Chinese works, which date back to the Chou and Han Dynasties (1122 B.C.–A.D. 220) show the tiger to have been an early object of worship. In the *I Ching* (The Book of Changes), the tiger assumes a role in astronomical and astrological tradition, appearing in the *Ssu Fang*, a map of the heavens showing special animals holding sway over the Four Directions of the Universe and the four seasons of the year:

Winter, North = Black Tortoise
Spring, East   = Blue Dragon
Summer, South = Vermilion Bird (Phoenix)
Autumn, West = White Tiger

The tiger was put in charge of the autumn season because his fierceness seemed to match the fierceness of this season in northern China. (The tiger's autumn ferocity was attributed to the fact that this was the animal's mating season, during which he roamed restlessly abroad seeking a mate.) At this early period, the tiger also took his place in the animal zodiac.

Another reason for venerating the tiger and marking him out as "king of beasts" is that the dark markings on his forehead resemble the Chinese character *wang* (王), meaning "royal."

The common striped tiger was said to live an incredible number of years, becoming a white tiger when he reached the age of five hundred, and becoming immortal at one thousand—at which time he also gained the power to transform himself into any shape whatever.

The tiger and the dragon also represented wind and water, and so played important roles in *Feng-Shui*, the ancient pseudoscience that determined the natural spots most propitious for an ancestral grave or for the erection of a temple, home, or business. The tiger and the dragon also represented the *yin* and *yang* forces of nature. The tiger, depicting the *yin*, or material force, roars at the dragon, representing the *yang*, or spiritual force. This was interpreted as a contest between wind and water. The wind, which follows the tiger, blows vigorously into the clouds, which follow the dragon. According to the *I Ching:* "The breath of the tiger creates the wind and the breath of the dragon creates the clouds; together they create the rain, which fructifies the earth and brings forth food for mankind." In times of drought, therefore, it became customary to drop the tiger's bones into the dragon's well, an act so enraging the dragon that he caused a storm cloud to form, resulting in a heavy rainfall.

Early Taoism considered the tiger to represent the force of darkness. Buddhism, coming later, transformed the beast into the symbol of power, grandeur, and glory. In northern China, where the tiger was rare, the simple country folk called him *Ta Sheng*, the Great Spirit, and attributed supernatural powers to him. In the South, where indeed he was known all too well, for he often preyed upon the villages, the tiger was dreaded as a menace to human life. The tiger appeared in early Chinese art on bronze and pottery vessels, usually in hunting scenes, and both as the hunted animal and on a leash for use in the chase.

In Japan the tiger was not known at all, and so, after he was introduced with the dragon from China, he was depicted in art as a rather mythical creature, not scientifically drawn (any more than was the Chinese or Cambodian lion). The depictions expressed the Japanese concept of a lofty spiritual idea. The story is told that when a westerner once criticized a Japanese artist for his unrealistic drawing of a tiger, the artist replied: "Yes, possibly this is true. But it is morally perfect!" He had drawn the powerful spirit of the tiger, not his body.

Because the tiger represented such strength, it was felt that he had the power to destroy any other animal by absorbing into himself their evil qualities, thereby rendering them powerless. From this idea grew the notion that any part of the tiger's body could be used as a fetish. So tiger claws and bones, both real and reproduced, were carried about as amulets to ward off calamity and to inspire the weak with tiger courage. Tiger charms were always worn by warriors and fastened to weapons. The tiger skin was worn by heroes deemed worthy of that honor. On buildings of all kinds, the image of the tiger could ward off entry by any species of demon. A tiger painting on a screen at the entrance to a magistrate's hall was guaranteed to strike terror and repentance into the heart of any culprit. In our own times, to call an enemy a "paper tiger" is to imply cowardice.

Medicines concocted of pulverized tiger bones and teeth, mixed with the animal's gall, were considered a special dosage to instill tiger strength in a man. Tiger bristles were held to be poisonous. But tiger talismans, worn or held close to the body, could cure almost any ailment.

The Year of the Tiger is, then, a year for great deeds of strength and courage, a year for daring. It is an especially good year for boys, since male children fortunate enough to be born in the Year of the Tiger will be strong, brave, aggressive, active. As extra insurance, some parents add to their son's name the word for tiger! But since girls born in that year are thought to be headstrong and obstinate (traits considered unwomanly in the Orient), parents would prefer that their daughters be born in another year. Furthermore, tiger-year girls run a high risk of leaving their husbands, since the tiger can run a thousand miles in one night and back again! But does this mean that tiger-year boys will also stray? Tradition does not say. Since the tiger year would seem to be propitious for creation of the new woman of the Women's Liberation Movement, it may well be that a new tiger tradition is even now in the making.

Tiger people are thoughtful, sensitive, sympathetic, but prone to indecision and quick temper. They are likely to be of a suspicious nature and don't easily trust others. They can be stubborn, selfish, narrow-minded, and bad-tempered. But the tiger does symbolize protection over human life, so during this year the "three disasters" of thieves, fire, and ghosts will be held at bay.

Tiger-born people should try to marry those born in the year of the horse, dragon, or dog. If they can't find anyone there, let them try someone from the rat, ox, rabbit, tiger, sheep, cock, or boar years. But *never* a snake- or a monkey-year mate!

 The rabbit bests the tiger

The rabbit used to love to play tricks on the tiger. Often he was able to outwit this lord of the forest.

One day a rabbit was foraging for food near the edge of the jungle. He was so absorbed in what he was doing that he didn't notice the approach of a tiger, who got close enough to capture the rabbit. Thinking quickly how he might make his escape, the rabbit offered a suggestion to his captor:

"If you spare my life, I'll not only give you the fine

drum that my late father left me, but I'll teach you to play it, too."

The tiger thought it would be much more interesting to play a drum than to eat one small rabbit. So he agreed to the plan, and the two animals then ran together to the foot of a lemon tree. There the rabbit pointed out to the tiger a beehive hanging from a low branch. "There you are," said he. "This is the drum I told you about. To play it, just insert your tail into that hole in the bottom, and then move it around. You can play it just as long and as often as you like. But one thing you must remember. The drum can be played only when I'm away from it. So I'll leave now, and I'll call out to you when it's all right for you to start playing."

Whereupon the rabbit rushed away. In a few moments the tiger heard the rabbit shout, and so he backed around and thrust his tail into the hole in the bottom of the beehive, then moved it around with some force. Sure enough, he immediately heard a sound, but it was that of the bees, who rushed angrily out and stung the poor tiger painfully, all over his body. The astonished animal fled from this assault, nearly dead from shock and pain. The next day, when he had recovered somewhat, he determined to take his revenge upon the rabbit.

So he started searching every nook and cranny of the forest for the culprit. At noon he caught up with him. The rabbit pleaded total innocence and claimed that the bees must have somehow appropriated his drum without his being aware of it. He gave the tiger fresh assurances:

"Just calm down, sir, and I'll give you the violin that my grandfather left me."

Once again the tiger was taken in, and he followed the

rabbit to a bamboo grove. The rabbit showed him what he should do to play the violin (after he, the rabbit, should have disappeared). The tiger listened attentively, nodded, and then, when the rabbit shouted back that it was all right to proceed, the tiger put his tail between two bamboos and waited for the wind to blow to make beautiful music. At last the breeze stirred and the bamboo branches were blown close together, emitting a lovely, soft sound. But the tail of the tiger, caught between the two bamboos, was ground and cut. Once again the tiger howled with pain and rage, gingerly pulled his tail from the trap, and set out in pursuit of the rabbit.

The rabbit saw his enemy coming after him, and he ran so fast that he fell into a deep pit. It was too deep for him to jump clear. "Now I've really had it!" he thought. But once again he devised a scheme. When the tiger got to the edge of the pit and looked down at the trapped rabbit, the latter threatened him, saying: "The sky is about to fall down and crush you to pieces, but I'm not going to permit you to share my shelter. You're too bad-tempered!"

Without pausing to think, the tiger jumped into the pit. There he caught the rabbit, and, to get even with him (as he thought), he threw the little fellow out. How happy the rabbit was! Out in the clear, he peered in his turn down at the tiger in the pit, and he said: "The sky isn't going to fall down at all! I'm going to fetch the villagers to come catch you."

And, since the pit was too deep for him to jump out of, the poor tiger had to sit there and await his fate!

*   *   *

Because tigers are animals that inhabit the mountain regions, and are therefore well known to the Vietnamese, tiger stories are numerous in that land. I heard many of them from my students at the university, as we all sweated out the strange English language, with frequent lapses into French.

Why the tiger has dark stripes

Long, long ago, the tiger was a very beautiful creature indeed, famous for his immaculate and sleek yellow coat and his matching amber-colored eyes. Truly, the tiger was the most elegant creature in the whole forest!

But one day, such a tiger was observing a nearby field from a grove at the edge of a mountain. In the field a farmer was ploughing with his buffalo. The toiling beast had become so exhausted that his mouth was dripping froth and his tongue hung out as he panted for breath. Still the farmer spurred him on, beating him with a stick and shouting at him to make greater effort.

Seeing this mistreatment of a fellow animal, the tiger became furious. Cannily, he waited until the farmer had stopped for lunch and gone away to get refreshment. Then, approaching the buffalo, the tiger scolded him for his stupid endurance. "You're far bigger and stronger than man," declared the tiger. "You have a huge body and two sharp horns to defend yourself with. Why then do you take such abuse? Why don't you stand up to this puny little fellow who takes such advantage of you?"

"It's quite true that the man is physically smaller than I am," replied the buffalo. "But he has a keen intelligence with which he can control all things in nature, even strong beasts like you and me."

Now the tiger had never heard of a weapon called a keen intelligence, and he was extremely interested to know what it looked like. So he sat on the dike and waited for the farmer to return from his lunch.

"Say there, you, man," he cried when the farmer came back. "Your buffalo tells me that you have a keen intelligence. Please let me see what it is. Where do you keep it?"

"I don't happen to have it with me," said the farmer. "I usually keep it at home."

"Do go home and get it," urged the tiger. "Fetch it here so that I can see it!"

"I would do that," replied the farmer. "But I'm afraid that if I do, you will kill and eat my buffalo while I am gone. If you'll agree to let me bind you to the trunk of that tree over there, I'll go on home and get my intelligence and bring it back to show you; then I'll unfasten you."

So the tiger, being a credulous creature, permitted the man to fasten him securely to the tree with some wide, strong ropes.

But once he had immobilized the animal, the farmer began to gather straw and twigs, instead of starting home. He piled the straw and twigs around the tiger and then set them afire, exclaiming: "Here is my intelligence! Do you understand it now?"

The poor tiger, straining with all his might and main, burst his bonds and fled away into the forest, but not before the part of his fur between the ropes had been burned black. Ever since then he has worn black and yellow stripes, and has had a pretty good idea of man's intelligence!

*   *   *

Of all the tiger stories told me by my students in Vietnam this one has always remained my favorite. The poor, sweating buffalo, the curious tiger, and the clever farmer somehow come to life in this tale.

 ## The tale of the tiger and the mouse

Once upon a time a small mouse chanced to run close to the spot where an enormous tiger was sitting taking the sun. The tiger, lazily opening his great amber eyes, saw the tiny mouse, stretched out his huge paw with its great curved claws, and immediately had the terrified rodent at his mercy.

Shaking with fright, the mouse pleaded for his life with this giant of the forest: "Oh, great sir, please take pity upon me and do not kill me! I'm so very tiny that I would make the barest morsel of food for you, hardly an appetizer. But to my own family, I am very important. They will suffer greatly if they lose me, I assure you!"

The tiger was relaxed in the sunlight and really not very hungry at that moment, so he decided to be magnanimous. "All right, then, little one," said he. "Run away home and be happy with your family!"

At the same time he loosened his clutch and the mouse stepped daintily to the ground. Once free, however, he did not immediately turn and scamper away. Turning back to his captor, he said politely and sincerely: "Thank you, thank you! Never for a moment will I forget that in your great kindness you spared my life. To repay you for the good you have shown me, I am certain that in future you will receive only good!"

Then he ran away as fast as he could, scuttling back to his family nest several hundred yards away, where he was warmly received by his wife and children, especially after they had heard of his close brush with disaster.

Not too long after this event, it happened that the tiger—the very same tiger—was caught in a snare set by hunters in the deepest part of the forest. By chance, the same little gray mouse happened to pass by. Seeing the tiger's plight, the mouse scampered quickly home and summoned his whole family, including distant cousins, to come help. With all their sharp little teeth working busily, the whole mouse family gnawed through the ropes binding the tiger to the trap. In a short time, the tiger was set free. You can well imagine his gratitude to his former captive and his family, as well as the pride of the mouse family in having repaid its debt to the great monarch of the jungle!

These events taught the animals that no act of kindness is ever wasted in this life, and that sometimes even those who are humbler, weaker, and generally more helpless than we are can assist us mightily when we are in danger or need.

It is a wise human being who learns this lesson early in life!

* * *

This is a story of two animals well known in Vietnam, and one told to me by my university students. More important, it is a story that teaches a Confucian concept reverently held by Asians: the value of an act of kindness that will be repaid when least expected, and often when most needed.

The faithful tiger

The events of this story are said to have taken place during the period when Vietnam was ruled by the Chinese. Some of these conquerors from the north treated the Vietnamese with great cruelty. Many of the Vietnamese lost their lives.

Sir Le Minh, a high Vietnamese official, whose wife and sons had been put to death and whose soldiers had been jailed, was forced to flee into the forest to escape persecution.

In the wildest and most desolate part of the jungle, Le Minh built himself a small hut from tree branches and leaves. In this hut he lived alone, in sorrow and deep despair. He was certain that he would never be given opportunity to seek revenge.

In order to earn a meager living, Le Minh cut and sold wood. Every morning, very early, he took his axe and went out deeper into the forest. After he had set to work on one particular morning, he heard a sudden and terrible scream of anguish. Searching the area for its source, he discovered a large tiger pinned under a fallen tree. The poor distraught animal had been trying to escape, but the trunk was too heavy. At once Le Minh cut away the tree trunk and freed the animal. In his great joy and relief, the animal frisked about, then bowed to his rescuer, turned, and ran away.

The next morning, just as usual, Sir Le Minh left his hut to go to work in the forest. To his astonishment, he saw lying in front of his doorway some dead rabbits and a deer. Carrying them to the market, he was able to sell them for a good price. From that day forward, he discovered dead game in front of his hut each morning. Selling it at the market provided him with a good deal of money, and his life became much easier.

One morning, to his amazement, he found in front of his hut not only dead animals, but also a number of dead Chinese! Le Minh realized that someone, somehow, was carrying out his revenge for him, and this made him very happy. He set about to bury the dead Chinese, but, as he was doing so, a troop of Chinese soldiers discovered him. Accused as the murderer, and unable to prove his innocence, Sir Le Minh was put to death.

That night the silence of the forest was broken by a loud, anguished, piercing scream. Once again, it was the tiger's scream, but this time not because he had met with an accident. This time he screamed because his benefactor, Le Minh, had been killed. Digging a large hole in the ground, the tiger tenderly buried his friend's body.

Then, tracking down the Chinese soldiers who had killed Le Minh, the tiger destroyed them. Five days later, he buried them beside the grave of the Vietnamese hero. Thus did the faithful tiger repay the man who had befriended him and saved his life.

After that, every night of the year, people living in that area heard the howls of the tiger as he mourned his benefactor. Then, one night, the mourning cries ceased and were heard no more. In his turn, the tiger had died. His body was discovered lying pressed on the grave of Sir Le Minh.

*   *   *

Loyalty is another Confucian virtue held in high regard by the Vietnamese, as they learned it over a thousand years ago from Chinese masters who left their cultural imprint on their land. Here the tiger, known in Vietnam more than in other South Asian lands, reveals his ability to remain loyal unto death to his benefactor.

4 THE HARE

卯 兔

MAO   T'U

The Hare

The hare (or rabbit) is well known throughout all of Asia, as indeed it is in most parts of the world, and a number of Oriental traditions have grown up around it. One has it that the female hare conceives by licking the coat of the male. Another claims that she conceives as the direct result of gamboling in sea breakers in the full moonlight on the eighteenth day of the eighth month. Other traditions attribute her conception to merely gazing at the moon!

This association of the hare and the moon is common to folklore all over the world. It is said the Hottentots tell the tale of how death came to the world through a mistake made in the hare's carrying a message to the moon! (Can it be that "hare" and "message" are symbolic of modern scientific techniques, and that the Hottentots have ESP?)

In India, ancient Sanskrit inscriptions suggest that the hare was associated with primitive cults whose adherents saw a resemblance between the animal and the visible markings on the moon. The twelve zodiacal gods of the Brahmans include a moon *deva* named Soma, or Chandra, who holds a white hare and reposes on a crescent moon.

One of the most beloved Buddhist legends comes from among the Buddha birth tales that originated in India. This story relates that Sakyamuni, the Buddha, was once incarnate as a hare. In this guise, he nobly sacrificed himself to ease the hunger pangs of the disguised god Indra. In gratitude, Indra then put the figure of the animal on the moon to commemorate this act of great virtue.

The Chinese apparently inherited the Indian traditions, for even before the Han Dynasty, records claimed that the hare derives his origin from the moon's vital essence, is always subject to the moon's influence, and indeed inhabits the moon. Later, the Taoists claimed that a large white hare serves Ch'ang-O, the queen of the moon, and compounds the elixir of life for her.

The Chinese always looked upon the appearance of a white hare as an auspicious omen, foretelling the reign of a beneficent and just ruler. It was believed that the white hare had to live one thousand years before he acquired his gleaming coat, and was therefore divine. (At the age of five hundred, the hare's coat was said to become blue.) Tradition held that in the golden age of the great Chou Dynasty, white hares had frisked about the streets of Ch'ang-an, the capital city. From those remote times on, it was customary, when a white hare was found, to capture him and deliver him to the emperor.

Not all divine hares are necessarily white. Ancient Chinese writings describe a red hare that, together with the phoenix and the unicorn, appears as harbinger of peace and prosperity. A black hare was also welcome. Chang Ssu-wei once wrote:

The black hare is more uncommon than the white hare. It comes from the North Pole, bringing greetings from the moon goddess, and is auspicious of a successful reign. Now may the magic medicine be pounded with a jade pestle and the divine nectar be prepared in a crystal cup.

The hare and the moon legend migrated from China to Japan; but there, instead of compounding a magic potion, he is said to perform the more practical duty of pounding rice in preparation of the food that is the real elixir of life! The substitution is said to have occurred as a result of a Japanese homophone, in which the characters for "full moon" and "rice cake" have the same sound. The Japanese also claim that the hare has the task of keeping the moon clean and bright, which he does by polishing it constantly with handfuls of horsetail plants.

In China the hare is prized for his speed, and as an unusual source of extremely fine hair from which writing brushes are made. The hair of the rabbit is taken in the fall, when his down is most delicate, and since it is made into the finest writing brushes, it has become traditional in Japan to do the first writing of the new year with a new brush made of rabbit hair.

In northern Japan, the Ainu held the rabbit to possess an evil eye with which to cast spells upon people. The rabbit's foot, of course, is widely held to be a countercharm against witchcraft, a fetish to forestall evil and bring good luck.

Tales of the rabbit's cunning are worldwide. In

some places it is thought that to eat the flesh of this animal is to become inculcated with his timidity, and so it is shunned as food.

"Hare days" figure in Japanese tradition. The *mayudama,* a sort of Christmas tree decorated with cakes in honor of the silkworm, appears on whatever day in January happens to be the "first day of the hare." On the first day of the tenth month there is a unique celebration in Kishu Province called "The Laughing Festival of Wasa." It comes from the legend that October, the tenth month, is often called the "godless month" because at that time all the deities have a reunion at the Izumo Shrine. It is said that when this meeting was first called, one deity made a mistake in the date and didn't show up until the session was ending. Naturally, the other gods all laughed at him. The Wasa festival, commemorating that human error by a divinity, is a time of "merriment from morning until evening."

The rabbit year is a fine year to be born in. People born in the Year of the Hare are always happy (since they always accept their fate meekly, whatever it may be). They are rather timid people, a bit weak, and rather easily led by stronger characters. But they have lovable personalities and are generally liked. They are ambitious and talented but will probably never become leaders. They are smooth talkers, a bit prone to gossip, but tactful and unwilling to hurt people. They have ambition; they are virtuous, clever at business, and financially astute. They are conservative and tend to look before they leap.

Temperamentally, they are somewhat given to melancholy, and can weep easily. They tend to be pedantic, well-informed on some subjects of interest but lacking in really inquiring minds, so that they do not blaze new trails. However, they make excellent gamblers, because they possess an uncanny instinct for picking a sure thing! They never lose their tempers except under prolonged provocation. Their temperaments are placid and unruffled.

Those born in the hare year should try to marry someone born in the year of the sheep, the boar, or the dog. A person born in the Year of the Dragon will not prove a good match, and a rabbit-year individual must absolutely shun mating with anyone from the years of the rat or the cock!

 The rabbit in the moon

There was once in a small kingdom a ruler named Ho-Yi. This Ho-Yi was a clever man, and said to be one of the finest archers in the world. One proof of this was a legend that in his youth there had been ten suns blazing in the sky, but that Ho-Yi, unassisted, had shot down nine of them, leaving only one.

Ho-Yi had a beautiful wife named Chang-O. This lady had been judged the prettiest girl in the whole kingdom, and Ho-Yi, entranced by her charms, had selected her himself as his queen. He loved her very much indeed. Unfortunately, Chang-O, who was repelled by what she considered her husband's rough and uncouth manners, did not return his affection at all.

One year, on the birthday of the Queen Mother of the Heavens, Ho-Yi went to call upon her and to offer his congratulations and good wishes. Pleased at this attention, the Queen Mother gave him as a gift a magic pill containing the elixir of immortality. On the homeward journey, King Ho-Yi got drunk with wine. As soon as he had reached his palace, therefore, he wanted to lie down and sleep, so he entrusted the pill to his wife for safe-keeping. Intrigued by the idea of its magic power, Chang-O swallowed the pill. At once she found herself floating on air, and discovered that if she wanted to, she could fly.

When Ho-Yi awakened, his first request was for the return of his pill. When Chang-O was unable to produce it, her husband threatened to kill her. As he advanced menacingly toward her, the unfortunate wife trembled with fear, but, remembering her newly discovered power, she managed to elude her fate by soaring off into the skies. Safely out of reach, she hid herself in a cave on the moon. Ho-Yi did pursue her, but he was stopped and turned back by the heavenly guard Wu-Kang. Defeated, the angry king returned to his earthly kingdom.

Since at that time there was no one in charge of the kingdom of the moon, the Queen Mother of the Heavens appointed Chang-O the mistress of the Palace of the Moon.

One day, alone in her moon palace, Chang-O was seized with an uncontrollable fit of coughing. In the midst of it, she spat up the magic pill, which immediately turned into a large white hare. Chang-O was so angry at losing her magic pill that she produced a mortar and pestle and, handing these to the hare, demanded that he reproduce for her the lost pill. Later, Chang-O herself was turned into a three-legged toad, and to this day you can see them all there in the full moon, standing under the sacred cassia tree: the hare with the pestle in his forepaws, pounding out in his mortar the elixir of immortality, and beside him the lady Queen Chang-O, waiting for the pill she lost. At their feet squats the three-legged toad into which the spirit of Chang-O was later changed. Thus they have remained through the ages and thus they can be seen also in many decorative designs in Chinese art.

A thousand silver flakes from snowdrifts broken
Flutter in the autumn winds, beneath the white-faced moon.
The divine mushrooms and fragrant cinnamon wear a fleecy mantle.
The restless spirit of the jeweled hare is in the Jade Gate
Though his helpless body lies upon a golden tray.
Toward the fairy queen Chang-O he gazes,
Yearning for a magic draught of life.

*   *   *

The story "The Rabbit in the Moon" is one of the ancient Chinese classical legends. Perhaps we can say that it reveals some of the Chinese belief in both magic and immortality. The poem with which the tale ends is by the poet Hsieh Ch'eng-chi of the Ming Dynasty.

The white hare of Inaba

The deity who was Master of the Great Land had eighty deities who were his brothers. But these brothers all left the land of the deity Master of the Great Land, because each of the eighty longed to wed the Princess of Yakami in Inaba. So they went together to Inaba, putting their bag on the back of their half brother, the deity Great Name Possessor, whom they took along as their attendant. When they arrived at Cape Keta, they found a naked hare lying there. Then the eighty deities spoke to the hare, saying: "What thou shouldst do is to bathe here in the sea water and then lie on the slope of a high mountain exposed to the blowing of the wind." So the hare followed the instructions of the eighty deities, and bathed and lay down.

But as the sea water dried, the blowing of the wind caused the poor animal's skin to split, so that the hare lay weeping in pain. But the deity Great Name Possessor, who, burdened with the bag, came by last of all, saw the hare and said: 'Why liest thou weeping?'

The hare replied, saying: "I was on the island of Oki and wished to cross over to this land, but had no means of crossing. For this reason I deceived the crocodiles of the sea, saying: 'Let you and me compete and compute the numbers of our respective tribes. So do you go and fetch every member of your tribe and make them all lie in a row across from this island to Cape Keta. Then I will tread upon them and count them as I run across.

Hereby we shall know whether it or my tribe is the larger.'

"Upon my speaking thus, they were deceived and lay down in a row and I trod upon them and counted them as I ran across, and I was just about to get on land when I turned and said: 'You have been deceived by me!' As soon as I had uttered these words, the crocodile who lay last of all seized me and stripped off all my clothing. As I was weeping and lamenting for this reason, the eighty deities who went by commanded and exhorted me, saying: 'Bathe in the salt water and then lie down exposed in the wind.' So in doing as they had instructed me, my whole body was hurt!"

Thereupon the deity Great Name Possessor instructed the hare, saying: "Go quickly now to the river mouth, wash thy body with the fresh water, then take the pollen of the sedges growing at the river mouth, spread it about, and roll about upon it, whereupon thy body will certainly be restored to its original state."

So the hare did exactly as it was instructed, and its body became as it had been originally. This was the white hare of Inaba. It is now called the hare deity.

So the hare said to the deity Great Name Possessor: "Those eighty deities shall certainly not get the Princess of Yakami. Though thou bearest the bag, Thine Augustness shall obtain her."

Thereupon the Princess Yakami, who was at that moment answering the eighty deities, was moved to respond, saying: "I will not listen to your words. I mean to marry the deity Great Name Possessor."

So the eighty deities, becoming enraged and wishing to slay the deity Great Name Possessor, took counsel together, on arriving at the foot of Mt. Tema in the Land of Hahaki, and said to the deity Great Name Possessor:

"On this mountain there is a red boar. So when we drive it down, do thou wait and catch it. If thou do not wait and catch it, we will certainly slay thee!"

Having thus spoken, they ascended the mountain, where they took fire and burned a large stone like unto a boar, and then rolled it down. Then as they drove it down and the deity Great Name Possessor caught it, he got stuck to and burned by the hot stone, and so he died.

Thereupon Her Augustness his august parent cried and lamented and went up to Heaven, and entreated His Divine Producing Wondrous Augustness, who at once sent Princess Cockleshell and Princess Clam to bring the dead deity back to life.

Then Princess Cockleshell triturated and scorched her shell and Princess Clam carried water and smeared the dead god as with mother's milk, whereupon he became a beautiful young man and wandered off.

Hereupon the eighty deities, seeing this, again deceived the deity Great Name Possessor, taking him with them into the mountains, where they cut down a large tree, inserted a wedge in the tree, and made him stand in the middle, whereupon they took away the wedge and tortured him to death.

Then Her Augustness his august parent, again seeking him with cries, she finally perceived him, and at once cleaving the tree, took him out and restored him to life once more, and said to him: "If thou remainest here, thou wilt at last be destroyed by the eighty deities."

So she sent him swiftly off to the august palace of the deity Great House Prince in the Land of Ki. Then, when the eighty deities searched and pursued him till they came upon him, and fixed their arrows in their bows, he escaped them by dipping under the fork of a tree and disappearing.

After other great adventures in the Nether Distant Land, the deity Great Name Possessor was eventually reunited with the Princess Yakami, who bore him a male child called the Deity of the August Wells.

* * *

The age-old tale "The White Hare of Inaba" is one of Japan's classics, recounted in the *Kojiki*, the historic record of ancient Japan. Its events are said to symbolize ancient tribal rivalries. Its retelling here is in the ancient classical style.

How the hare bested the wolf

One day, in the upper part of a Tibetan valley, high above the cultivated fields, a hungry wolf was prowling about searching for something to eat. All at once he came upon a rather delicious-looking donkey, about a year old. At once the wolf proceeded to stalk the donkey, thinking that he would make an excellent meal from him.

Just as he was about to seize him, the donkey noticed his approach and addressed him as follows: "Oh, Uncle Wolf, it is surely no good your eating me now. This is the springtime, and after the long, hard winter I am still very thin. If you will but wait for a few months, until next autumn, you will find me twice as fat as I am now, and I shall make you a much better feast."

"Very well," replied the wolf. "I will wait until then, on condition that you meet me on this spot in six months' time."

And so saying, he galloped off in search of some other prey.

In no time at all, the leaves had turned and autumn had come round. One fine morning, exactly six months later, the wolf started off to meet the donkey at the appointed spot. As he was loping along, drooling with anticipation, he came upon a fox.

"Good morning, Brother Wolf," said the fox. "Where are you off to this fine brisk morning?"

"Oh," replied the wolf, "I am going into the valley where I have an appointment with a donkey. I have an engagement to eat him this very day."

"How pleasant for you, Brother Wolf," answered the fox. "But as the donkey is such a large animal, you will scarcely be able to eat him all by yourself without getting a bad case of indigestion. I think you should let me accompany you and share in your feast."

The wolf was in a hospitable mood. "Certainly, Brother Fox," he replied. "I'll be glad to have your company."

So the two went on together. After they had proceeded a short distance, they came upon a hare.

"Good morning, Brother Wolf and Brother Fox," said the hare in greeting. "Where are you going this lovely day?"

"Good morning, Brother Hare," replied the wolf. "I am just going off into yonder valley to keep an appointment with a fat donkey whom I have arranged to eat for my dinner today. Brother Fox is coming along with me as my guest."

"Oh, really, Brother Wolf?" responded the hare. "Well, I do wish you would ask me along, too. A donkey is really too large for even the two of you, and you could well afford to let such a small creature as I share in a bit of the spoil."

"Why, certainly, Brother Hare," replied the wolf, who was in a mellow mood. "We shall be delighted to have you accompany us."

And so the three animals went on together to the appointed spot. When they approached the place, they saw the young donkey waiting for them. During the summer months he had consumed a quantity of grass and had become fat and sleek, almost twice as big as he had been in the spring. When the wolf caught sight of him he could scarcely contain his delight and began to lick his chops in anticipation.

"Well, Brother Donkey," he said affably. "Here I am, according to our agreement, ready to eat you. I am happy to see you looking so plump and well. Here are Brother Fox and Brother Hare who have come along with me for a bite to eat."

And so saying, the wolf crouched down, ready to spring upon the donkey.

"Wait a moment, Brother Wolf," called out the hare at this moment. "I have a suggestion to make. It seems to me it would be a pity for you to kill this fine young donkey in the usual way, by seizing his throat, for, if you do, a great deal of his blood will be wasted. I should like to suggest, as a better plan, that you strangle him, for in that situation no blood will be lost, and we shall then derive the full benefit from his carcass."

The wolf straightened up and thought this over. Then he said: "Well, Brother Hare, that's an excellent idea. I wonder why I didn't think of it myself. But how is it to be done?"

"Easily enough," answered the hare. "Over yonder is a shepherd's encampment. There we can borrow a rope, in which we will make a slipknot, put the loop over the donkey's head, and pull as hard as we can."

So they all agreed on this plan. Brother Fox was dispatched to the encampment to borrow a rope from the shepherd, and he carried it back to where his companions were waiting.

"Now," said the hare, "here is our procedure. We will put this large slipknot over the donkey's neck, and as he is so large and heavy, we must all three pull together at the other end of the rope. So you, Brother Wolf, and you, Brother Fox, put your heads through these smaller loops I have fixed; I will seize the loose end of the rope with my teeth, and when I give the signal, let us all pull together."

The other two fell in with this plan at once. So they threw the slipknot over the donkey's neck and the wolf and the fox put their heads through the smaller loops. When they were all ready, the hare took up his position at the end of the rope, and caught hold of it with his protruding front teeth.

"Now," said he, "are you ready?"

"Yes, ready," answered the wolf.

"Yes, quite ready," echoed the fox.

"Well, then, pull," said the hare.

So they began to pull, just as hard as they could. When the donkey felt the pull on the rope, he walked forward a few paces, much to the surprise of the wolf and the fox, who felt themselves being dragged along the ground.

"Pull, can't you!" shrieked the wolf, as the rope began to tighten around his neck.

"Pull yourself!" shrieked back the fox, who was now beginning to feel very uncomfortable, with the blood pounding in his forehead.

"Pull, all of you," called out the hare, and with that, he let go of the end of the rope, and the donkey galloped off, dragging the fox and the wolf after him. In a few moments, both were strangled soundly. The donkey, shaking off the rope from his neck, pulled back his lips and gave one loud "hee-haw" up the valley. Then he proceeded to graze quietly in his usual pastures.

The hare twitched his nose in amusement, then scampered off home, feeling that he had done an admirable day's work.

*   *   *

Many Asian tales love to relate the besting of a larger, more powerful animal by a smaller, weaker, but cleverer one. This seems to be a mark of human nature! "How the Hare Bested the Wolf" comes from Tibet.

5 THE DRAGON

辰　龍

CH'EN　LUNG

The Dragon

 The dragon represents the highest celestial power and, with the tiger, is one of the two most beneficent astrological influences. The dragon is the only mythical animal in the Asian animal zodiac, an indication of its importance. It represents fire, authority, and power; the *yang* (or male) element in nature; the first cause.

The concept of the dragon probably emerged in earliest times from among a primitive people who worshipped serpents and the sun, and who sought answers to the basic questions of the existence of this planet and of the presence of man on it. Such introspection led people to symbolic representation of their philosophic concepts. Thus the "Four Directions" were represented by the Blue Dragon of the East, the Black Tortoise of the North, the Vermilion Bird (Phoenix) of the South, and the White Tiger of the West. Another early concept was that of the "Four Fabulous Animals"—the dragon, who presided over heavenly authority; the phoenix, chief of all feathered birds; the unicorn, chief of all hairy animals; and the tortoise, chief of all animals with shells. These animals, together with naked man, constituted the five tribes of the quinary system of the ancient Chinese.

Since the dragon is a mythical creature, he is composed of the most imposing and powerful characteristics of some known animals. The dragon is thought to have the head of a camel with the horns of a deer (his hearing and flying abilities stem from his horns); the ears of an ox; the eyes of a hare, with extra-heavy eyebrows; a beard with long, streaming bristles; lengthy tusks; and a serpent-like body covered with the shining scales of the carp, topped with a bristling row of dorsal spines extending to and about the mouth (which is large). The dragon's lengthy body terminates in a tail like a serpent's, with a series of sharply pointed fins; his four short, bowed legs end in feet that combine the paw of a tiger and the talons of a hawk. Flamelike appendages emanate from the shoulders and the hips. His claws vary in number according to country and rank. In Japan, the dragon is usually depicted with three claws. In China, the ordinary everyday dragon had four claws, but the special dragon for the imperial household had five. The dragon's body scales are limited to nine times nine (the luckiest possible number). The scales of his neck are placed in the reverse position of those on the body.

In his mouth the dragon holds the magic pearl always associated with him. When paper dragons are carried in festival processions in Asia, a man usually runs ahead of the animal holding a white ball, representing the pearl, which the dragon tries to grasp. The meaning of the pearl, or ball, is not clear. It may represent the moon: since the moon's appearance just before the rising of the Dragon Star announces the coming of the Chinese, or lunar, New Year, the period when the moon is just out of reach of the dragon's claws would be the time of spring and of new life, a time of hope. Or it may represent the sun, the most powerful heavenly body, and one that is therefore closely associated with the dragon. But some people cling to the belief that the ball represents a jewel in which is encased the spiritual essence or the operating principle of the universe.

About the body of the dragon whirl countless nebulae, and his breath emerges from his nostrils in a mixture of fire and steaming water, which are converted into spiraling clouds, symbolizing the great cosmic forces.

Like its power, the dragon's wisdom exceeds that of all other animals; he is empowered to transform himself into any size or shape whatsoever, whether it be that of a tiny silkworm or a beast large enough to cover the whole earth and darken the entire sky!

The dragon may have emerged from men's minds because of their knowledge of the Indian *naga* (see p. 108). Taoism endowed the dragon with magic properties, while Buddhism gave him spiritual qualities as a protector of divinities and a guardian of temples. The dragon could bring good or evil, so that he must be both worshipped and propitiated. Some people believed that the dragon emerged originally out of a great storm; others that he was a real creature who had coexisted with man for millions of years.

His inclusion in the Asian animal zodiac with eleven real animals indicates that at least some people thought him to be real. According to one Japanese legend, the dragon originated in an egg the size of an ostrich egg: the foetus, a small snake, was encased in a shell of heavy stone that must lie dormant at the bottom of the sea for a thousand years. At the end of that time, the egg would float to the surface of the sea, where, attracted by its beautiful colors, someone would pick it up and place it on land. There it must rest for another thousand years until the proper moment came for the enclosure to split spontaneously and the small snake to emerge. At once this snake would increase in size, generate a huge storm, and ascend into the heavens.

There are different species of dragons. Celestial dragons guard the mansions of the gods and support them against collapse. Spiritual dragons make the winds blow and produce rains to benefit mankind. Earth dragons mark the courses of rivers and streams. Dragons of hidden treasures guard wealth concealed from mortals. Sometimes dragons are subdivided into land, sea, and sky dragons. Dragons also come in assorted colors: red, violet, blue, green, yellow, white, black. The rain dragon is black; the dragons of mountains, caves, and marshes are amber-colored; the white dragon produces gold by blowing his breath upon the world; the violet dragon produces crystal balls from its drool; but best of all is the yellow dragon, because the dragon that emerged from the River Lo in ancient legend was yellow. The yellow dragon was the special protector of the emperor and the imperial household in China. The throne was referred to as the "dragon seat," and dragons were used to decorate imperial robes and furnishings.

The emperor's face was the dragon face, and his anger was "the reversal of the dragon's scales."

So the dragon has been a favorite and recurring theme in Asian art and legend. Stories are told of dragon paintings and carvings so wondrous that, once completed, the dragon wrenched himself from the canvas, wall, or ceiling, and vanished into the sky! Such a legend is recounted here in the story "Dotting the Dragon's Eye."

From the ancient *Nihongi* records, Japanese tradition recounts that the divine creator Izanagi, angered when his wife Izanami died in giving birth to the fire god Kagutsuchi, cut the child into three pieces, each of which promptly became a dragon!

A lovely Buddhist legend relates that Sakyamuni, while still seeking enlightenment, was walking in the mountains one evening and, looking down into a precipice, saw the Great Dragon, who knew the meaning of all things. The holy man, therefore, stopped and asked the dragon many questions whose answers he sought. All were answered satisfactorily. Then, in great and hushed expectation, the young prince propounded the ultimate question of the meaning of life and death, the single question whose answer he most wished to learn. The dragon replied that, before revealing this last great truth, he must have his endless hunger fed.

"I will bestow my own body for this purpose," answered the Holy One, without hesitation.

Thereupon the dragon revealed the sacred mystery, and Sakyamuni, true to his promise, hurled himself into the abyss toward the monster. Just as the dragon's great jaws were about to crush him, the dragon was transformed into a lotus blossom, which received the Buddha and bore him up to his former place on the mountain, where he continued his profound meditation for the alleviation of human suffering. This is why the Lord Buddha is usually depicted seated in contemplation on a lotus blossom.

So the dragon year is a wonderful year to be born into, especially for a boy. Like the year of the tiger, the dragon year is one of great deeds, high and lofty accomplishments. Dragon-year people are healthy, energetic, and brave. They are also honest and sensitive, dislike borrowing money, and inspire confidence. They are sincere, not given to idle talk or flattery. Their opinions are thoughtful and valid. Because they are tenderhearted, they are sometimes taken advantage of by unscrupulous people. They have large mouths, and are somewhat given to gossip, but are never hard or bitter in what they say. They tend to be excitable, and in that state may talk more than usual. They are capable of doing good work at whatever they undertake, and they often devote their energies to worthy causes. To be born in this year of the greatest celestial power is believed to endow people with the "four blessings": harmony, virtue, prosperity, and long life.

The person born in the dragon year should marry someone from the years of the monkey, rat, snake, or cock. Next best would be someone born in the years of the tiger, horse, ram, or boar. Marriage should be avoided with anyone from the ox, rabbit, or dragon years; and worst of all for a dragon person would be marriage with someone born in the Year of the Dog.

The dragon slayer

Once, when the world was young, Susano-o no Mikoto, a god dwelling in the heavens, was banished therefrom because of constant misbehavior. He descended to earth, to Torikami, beside the River Hi, in the province of Izumo.

The unfortunate creature found himself standing alone in a vast, desolate area, among bare trees and falling snow. Because he was a god, he did not feel hunger or thirst, but he did feel tiredness. So at night be would rest under a tree or beside a knoll and then, in the morning, resume his aimless wandering. Early one evening, when he was seeking shelter for the night, he saw a chopstick come floating down the stream, so he knew that people must be dwelling nearby. He set out to search for them and soon came upon an old man and an old woman who were weeping bitterly. Between them walked a lovely young woman of some seventeen summers.

"Who are you?" asked Susano-o, for his curiosity was aroused.

The old man answered him: "I am a god of earth, son of a mountain god, and my name is Ashinatsuchi; this woman is my wife, and her name is Tenatsuchi. The maiden is our daughter, named Kushinada-hime."

"Why do you weep?" asked Susano-o.

Said the old man: "We have had eight other daughters, but each year the dragon of Koshi has come and devoured one after the other. We weep now because the time is at hand for the dragon to come to claim our last remaining daughter."

"What is this dragon like?" asked Susano-o.

"Its eyes are as red as the winter cherry. Its body has nine heads and nine tails, and it is so long that it stretches over nine hills and nine valleys."

"If this maiden is your daughter," said Susano-o, "will you give her to me in marriage?"

"You honor me," replied the old man. "But I do not know your name."

"I am the dear brother of the sun goddess, and I have but recently descended from heaven."

"In that case, most obediently do I offer my daughter to you," the old man replied reverently.

Susano-o then transformed the girl into a comb, which he placed in the knot of hair at the nape of his neck. Then he bade the old couple to brew white wine (*sake*) and to fill nine jugs with it. He then requested that they build a fence with nine gates and nine benches, and told them to place on each bench a jar filled with the wine.

Soon the enormous dragon appeared, humping along the pathway, his scales gleaming in the sunlight, his nine necks craning in all directions, his nine noses blowing out steam and fire and causing a fearful windstorm. Soon the beast caught the scent of the *sake*. In no time at all, his nine huge months were emptying the nine vats. Nine minutes later he lay motionless, on top of the empty and overturned wine flagons. He had fallen sound asleep!

Approaching the dragon softly, the god Susano-o quickly cut off the creature's first head with his short sword. This unexpected shock awakened the dragon, who promptly blew his eight remaining noses in great rage and tried to focus his sixteen bloodshot eyes to locate his enemy. But in vain. The dragon was just too drunk to pick out any detail clearly!

So Susano-o was able to complete the task, killing the dragon and cutting him into small pieces. The River Hi ran red with blood.

When Susano-o cut the middle tail, his sword struck something hard and broke. He marveled much at this. Taking the point of his sword in his hand, he thrust and split the tail, and looked inside. There he found a most beautiful and wondrous sword. Susano-o took this sword out and kept it, later on sending it to his sister, the sun goddess Amaterasu at Ise. This sword is, in fact, the one called *Kusanagi-no-tachi* ("the herb-quelling dragon sword"). It is said to have a hilt composed of nine serpent rings and a blade decorated with marvelous dragons.

Susano-o later built a house in the land of Izumo, at a place called Suga. Clouds rose up about that place, forming an eightfold fence for husband and wife to retire behind, within the house. The maiden's father (who was now extremely happy) was appointed protector of the place.

And in this happy home, children were born to Susano-o and the young and lovely wife he had rescued from the dragon's jaws. Among these children were Otoshi-no-kami (Great Harvest Deity); Ukanomitama (the August Spirit of Food); and Onamuchi (the Great Name Possessor). It was this Onamuchi who was later involved with his eighty half brothers in the wooing of the Princess Yakami in Inaba, and who saved the white hare after his brothers had tricked it.

That story is told in the tale "The White Hare of Inaba."

*   *   *

The tale "The Dragon Slayer" is one of the most ancient Japanese stories. The hero, Susano-o no Mikoto, is one of the gods associated with the divine origin of the Japanese islands. It exists in many versions, some of which employ as hero and dragon-avenger a handsome young prince instead of the god.

The yellow dragon

This is the story of Wu, the son of a farmer named Yin, and how he won the favor of a dragon and rose to be a great man in China.

When Wu was a boy of thirteen, he was one day sitting at the garden gate, looking across the plain watered by a winding river flowing from the mountains. Wu was a silent, dreamy boy who had been reared by his grandmother, his mother having died when he was very young; and it was his habit to sit thus in silence, thinking and observing things.

On this particular day, there came suddenly along the highway a handsome youth riding a white horse. He was dressed, this young man, in yellow robes, and he appeared very definitely to be someone of high birth. He was accompanied by four manservants, one holding an umbrella to shield him from the sun's bright rays.

The youth drew up his horse at the gate and, addressing Wu, said: "Son of Yin, I am weary. May I enter your father's house and rest a little time?"

The boy bowed and replied: "Enter."

Yin then came forward and opened the gate. The noble youth dismounted and sat on a seat in the court, while his servants tethered the horse. The farmer chatted with his visitor, and Wu gazed at them silently. Food was brought, and, when the meal was finished, the youth thanked Wu for his hospitality, repeated his thanks to the farmer, and walked across the courtyard. Wu noticed that before one of the servants passed through the gate, he turned the umbrella upside down. When the youth had mounted his horse, he turned back to the silent, observant boy and said: "I shall come again tomorrow."

Wu bowed and answered: "Come."

The strangers then rode away, and Wu sat watching them until they had vanished from sight.

When evening came on, the farmer spoke to his son regarding the visitors, and said: "The noble youth knows my name, and yet I have never set eyes upon him before!"

For a time Wu was silent. Then he said: "I cannot say who the youth is, or who his attendants are."

"You watched them very closely, my son. Did you note anything unusual about them?"

Replied Wu: "There were no seams in their clothing; the white horse had spots of five colors and scaly armor instead of hair. The hooves of the horse and the feet of the strangers did not touch the ground."

In some agitation, Yin arose, exclaiming: "Then they are not human beings; they are spirits."

Said Wu: "I watched them as they went westward.

Rain clouds were gathering on the horizon, and when they were a great distance off, they all rose in the air and vanished in the clouds."

Yin was greatly alarmed to hear this, and said: "I must ask your grandmother what she thinks of this strange happening."

The old woman was fast asleep, and, as she had grown extremely deaf, it proved difficult to awaken her. When at length she was thoroughly aroused and sat up, her head and hands were trembling with palsy. Yin repeated to her in a loud voice all that Wu had told him.

Said the old woman: "The horse, spotted with five colors, and with scaly armor instead of hair, is a dragon horse. When spirits appear before human beings, they wear magic garments. That is why the clothing of your visitors had no seams. Spirits tread on air. As these spirits went westward, they rose higher and higher in the air, going toward the rain clouds. The youth was the Yellow Dragon. He is to raise a storm, and since he has four followers, the storm will be a great one. May no evil befall us!"

Then Yin told the old woman that one of the strangers had turned the umbrella upside down before passing through the garden gate. "That is a good omen," she said. Then she lay down and closed her eyes. "I have need of sleep," she murmured. "I am very old."

By this time heavy storm clouds were gathering in the sky, and Yin decided to sit up all night. Wu asked to be permitted to do the same, and his father consented. Then the boy lit a yellow lantern, put on the yellow robe that his grandmother had made for him, burned incense, and sat down to read charms from a yellow book.

The storm burst forth in fury just as dawn was breaking dimly. Wu then closed his yellow book and went to a window. The thunder bellowed, the lightning flamed, and the rain fell in torrents. Swollen streams overflowed their banks and poured down from the mountains. Soon the river near Wu's house rose in a flood and swept across the fields. Cattle gathered in groups on shrinking mounds that had become islands surrounded by raging water.

Yin feared greatly that the house would be swept away, and he wished that he had fled into the mountains.

At night the cottage was entirely surrounded by water. Trees were uprooted and swept away. "We cannot escape now," groaned Yin.

Wu sat in silence, displaying no emotion. "What do you think of it all?" asked his father.

Wu reminded him that one of the strangers had turned the umbrella upside down, and added: "Before the dragon youth went away, he spoke and said: 'I shall come again tomorrow.'"

"He has come indeed," Yin moaned, and he covered his face with his hands.

Said Wu: "I have just seen the dragon. As I looked toward the sky, he spread out his great hood above our home. He is protecting us now."

"Alas, my son, you are dreaming."

"But listen, father, no rain is falling on our roof!"

Yin listened intently. Then he said: "You speak truly, my son. This is indeed a great marvel."

"It was well," said Wu, "that you welcomed the dragon yesterday."

"He spoke to you first, my son; and you answered, 'Enter.' Ah, you have much wisdom. You will become a great man."

The storm began to subside, and Wu prevailed upon his father to lie down and sleep.

Much damage had been done by storm and flood, and large numbers of human beings and domestic animals had perished. In the village, which was situated at the mouth of the valley, only a few houses were left standing.

At midday, the rain ceased to fall. The sun then came out and shone brightly, so the waters began to retreat.

Wu went outside and sat at the garden gate, as was his custom. In time he saw the yellow youth returning from the west, accompanied by his four attendants. When he came close, Wu bowed, and the youth drew up his horse and spoke, saying: "I said I should return today."

Again Wu bowed respectfully.

"But this time I shall not enter the courtyard," the youth added.

"As you will," replied Wu politely.

The dragon youth then handed the boy a single scale which he had taken from the horse's neck, and said: "Keep this, and I shall remember you."

Then he rode away and vanished from sight.

The boy reentered the house. He awakened his father and said: "The storm is over and the dragon has returned to his pool."

Yin embraced his son, and together they went to inform the old woman. She awakened, sat up, and listened to all that was told her. When she learned that the dragon youth had again appeared and had spoken to Wu, she asked: "Did he give you something before he departed?"

Wu opened a small wooden box and showed her the

scale that had been taken from the neck of the dragon horse.

The woman was well pleased, and said: "When the emperor sends for you, all will be well."

Yin was astonished to hear these words, and he exclaimed: "Why should the emperor send for my boy?"

"You will see," the old woman answered him, as she lay down again.

Before very long the emperor himself did hear of the great marvel that had taken place in the flooded valley. Men who had taken refuge on the mountains had observed that no rain fell on Yin's house during the storm. So His Majesty sent couriers to the valley, and these men bade Yin and Wu accompany them to the palace.

When he was brought before the emperor, Yin related everything just as it had occurred. Then the emperor asked to be shown the scale of the dragon horse.

It was growing dark when Wu opened the box, and the scale shone so brightly that it illuminated the throne room, which became as bright as at high noon.

Said the emperor: "Wu shall remain here and become one of my magicians. The Yellow Dragon has imparted to him great power and wisdom."

Thus it came about that Wu attained high rank in the kingdom. He found that great miracles could be worked with the scale of the dragon horse. It cured disease and it caused the emperor's armies to win victories. Wu was able to foretell events with it, and, all in all, he became a renowned prophet and magician.

The farmer's son grew to be very rich and powerful. A great house was erected for him close to the royal palace, and he took his father and grandmother to it, and there they lived happily together to the end of their days.

Thus did Wu, son of Yin, become a great man, because of the favor done to him by the thunder dragon, who had wrought great destruction in the river valley and taken toll of many lives.

And from this simple tale, it can be seen that the Chinese dragon is not always a beneficent deity. Nor is he always an evil one. Like certain other gods, he is a destroyer and a preserver in one.

* * *

"The Yellow Dragon" is an ancient Chinese tale concerned with that imperial symbol, the mythical dragon, and revealing the yearning of simple people for magical power that might somehow transform them into rich and powerful figures.

 Dotting the dragon's eye

During the Southern Sung Dynasty (A.D. 1127–1279), in the State of Liang (near the present city of Nanking), there lived a certain Chiang, who was one of the three best-known painters of the Liang kingdom. He was, in fact, extremely famous for the high degree of his artistic skill revealed in his paintings. Since Buddhism was the prevailing religion of that period, Chiang painted, among other things, many murals in the Buddhist temples of the countryside.

One day the artist was visiting a famous temple called An-lo Shih. The abbot of that temple, recognizing Chiang and knowing his fame, asked him to consent to paint some of his famous murals to enhance the appearance of the temple's main hall, so that visitors might enjoy it more.

At first Chiang was reluctant to consent to do the work but because he found the abbot's flattery and persistence hard to resist, he finally agreed to the request. He went studiously to work and painted four large dragons on the walls. When they were completed, they looked so realistic that one could imagine they were truly alive. Their mouths were open, smoke and flame issued from them, and in truth it seemed as if, with a great roar, they might leave the walls altogether and disappear into the heavens. All the tourists and guests who visited the temple pavilion admired those paintings enormously— but they did notice one thing amiss. It seemed that Chiang had neglected to paint in the dragons' eyes!

So everyone requested that Chiang repair this oversight and paint in the eyes at once so that these marvelous dragons would be complete in every detail. To their surprise, Chiang refused, saying:

"I am not really trying to deny you your wish. The fact is that I ought not to paint eyes into those four dragons. For, once the eyes are there, the dragons will immediately burst through the walls and soar into the skies."

But the people refused to believe him. They decided that he must be snobbish, vain, conceited, in wanting the dragons to be left incomplete in this important detail. So they redoubled their pleas, and in the end Chiang was not able to face their insistence longer. So he picked up his brush and painted in one dragon's eyes—dotted the eyes in, as the Chinese say.

And lo! There was not even time for the abbot and the other people watching to praise the artist's work; the instant the eyes of the first dragon were in his head, those eyes suddenly moved! At that same moment, heaven and earth turned instantly dark. Thunder roared, and the hall was lit brightly by a flare of lightning. The thick temple wall burst asunder, top to bottom, and in one great glare of blinding light, the dragon left the wall, shot up into the clouds, and totally disappeared from view!

The other three dragons, their eyes not yet dotted in, remained quietly on their own walls. And there were no further requests from the people for Chiang to paint in the missing eyes!

This tale points up the fact that the real importance, the essence, of any artistic creation lies in defining the central point. Once that is captured, there is total insight. The creation comes alive!

*   *   *

The Chinese tale "Dotting the Dragon's Eye" has special interest for artists and people who love art, revealing as it does the important aesthetic point that the artistic creation lives only when perfectly completed. Indeed, it may also reveal another point in aesthetics that is particularly Asian: the value of that which is somehow slightly incomplete.

6 THE SNAKE

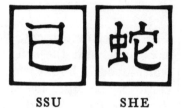

SSU   SHE

The Snake

The snake, or serpent, has long been associated with the sun, and has been worshipped in both eastern and western cultures. Because he sheds his skin, the snake symbolizes death and rebirth, life perpetually renewed and everlasting. This is akin to the rising and setting of the sun.

The snake's silence, stealth, slithering physique, his cunning and quickness, and the deadly venom he darts, all seem to make him a creature of mystery and supernatural power. His attraction to music—music which can lure him into captivity—and the ability of some species of snake to inflate a protective hood also seem to give the snake a special mystique which has been felt by many people for many ages. In India, the *naga*, a mythical seven- or nine-headed serpent, has been venerated from the time of the Vedas, although orthodox Brahmins never accepted the *naga*, but looked upon it rather as a demon.

But the *naga* came to have great significance in Buddhism because of the legend that when Gautama was sitting in meditation in the forest, before his enlightenment, a friendly serpent (the tutelary spirit of a nearby lake), wrapped his body seven times about the Holy One, spread his seven hoods protectingly over his head, and for seven days and seven nights guarded him against attack by other animals.

In China and Japan, and in the Oriental zodiac, the serpent is a creature totally distinct from the dragon. Within the zodiac, in fact, the serpent and the dragon represent not only different signs and years, but entirely opposite characteristics. The dragon symbolizes the positive, benevolent, constructive forces of the universe; the snake, those which are negative, malevolent, and destructive. The snake represents deceit and cunning, and, together with the tiger, the lizard, the centipede, and the three-legged toad, makes up the group called the Five Poisons!

The Chinese believe, in fact, that all human illnesses may come from snake poison, and, following an ancient theory that like cures like, they use remedies concocted of snake gall to heal sick people.

Perhaps the earliest example of psychosomatic sickness is described in the Ch'in dynasty legend telling about the relative of a man named Yueh Chuang who, while visiting him, thought he had swallowed a small snake which he saw in his wine cup. During the three years that followed this visit, he was very ill, and he attributed this condition to the drinking incident. Later on, he revisited Yueh Chuang and drank wine again from the same cup. This time he examined it closely, however, and discovered that the little snake was actually a reflection in the bowl of the cup from a painting on the ceiling. From that moment his sickness left him.

Women have always been associated with serpents, for some reason. Even the gentle Lord Buddha, who himself is said to have had several incarnations as a snake, likened women to the five types of dangerous snakes: the angry, the spiteful, the hateful, the ungrateful, and the venomous. In legend, snakes are often revealed to be real men or women under the spell of an enchantment.

In Japan, the goddess Benten is usually depicted in art with a snake, because she subdued a serpent that was devastating a village. This was in the vicinity of Enoshima Island, where the temple is now dedicated to Benten.

An ancient allegory connecting the snake, toad, and slug—"the three cringing ones"—is designed to teach the interdependence of all creatures and their balance of power over one another. A snake can swallow a toad; the toad can swallow the slug; but finally the slug, by covering its prey with a slimy secretion, can destroy the snake!

Snake figures were often used on god images, especially in Tibetan Buddhism, as symbolic ornaments (girdles, armlets, anklets, wristlets, headdresses). Their symbolization in this way represented the eternal revolution of ages and the succession, dissolution, and regeneration of mankind. Women who wear snake bracelets and rings today are probably not aware of that early significance.

Snake-year people are considered to be wise, profound, compassionate. They may also be vain, however, and overly interested in dress. They never have to worry about money, are unusually fortunate in their financial affairs, but tend to be careful about loaning money. Because snake people have a tendency to overdo everything, they can be annoying, even when they are trying to assist someone, because they then become overly solicitous. Snake people are determined and persistent, hate to fail in whatever they undertake, and prefer to rely on their own judgment rather than to seek the opinion of others. Although their natures are calm, they are intense. Snake-year people are often very beautiful, and this sometimes leads them into marital difficulties. They stray!

A person born in the year of the ox or the cock makes the best partner for someone born in the year of the snake. Second choice would be someone born in the years of the rat, hare, dragon, snake, horse, sheep, or dog. Marriage with someone born in the Year of the Monkey will prove a poor match, but the worst choice of all is someone born in the Year of the Tiger or the Year of the Boar.

 The deer and the snake

Long, long ago there was a great deluge, one such as had never been seen before by man. The River Dedong overflowed its banks and washed away many houses. All the fields became a vast lake, and all the inhabitants and their animals were drowned.

An old man in Pyongyang went rowing in the flood in a small boat. He found a deer almost exhausted and drowning, and he was able to rescue him. Then he found a snake floating on the waters, so he rescued him, too. Before long a boy came floating by, and the old man saved him as well. He then carried them all to the shore in his boat. There he released the deer and the snake. The boy would not leave the old man, however, since both his parents had been drowned and his home destroyed in the flood. So the old man gave him food to eat and adopted him as his son.

One day the deer came back and tugged at the old man's sleeve, swinging his tail from side to side. The old man guessed that he was trying to tell him something, and so he followed the animal. Before long they came to a rock in the mountains. The deer pawed the ground nearby, and the old man guessed that something must lie hidden there. He began to dig, and lo and behold, he found a jar full of gold and silver buried at that spot. He took the treasure home with him, and he was now a rich man!

But his foster son became very arrogant and began to spend money extravagantly. His father chided him for his recklessness, but the younger man often answered him rudely and took absolutely no heed of his admonitions. In the end, the youth decided that he would go away and live by himself, but his father refused to let him go. So the boy became angry and abusive, and even brought some false charges against his indulgent foster-father. He went secretly to the authorities and said: "My foster-father stole a lot of money, and he has made up some story that he got it from a deer! Can you imagine anything more ridiculous!"

The official responsible for such matters went to the old man and arrested him. This official absolutely refused to pay heed when the poor prisoner accounted for his wealth. The old man was flung into prison, but he always expected confidently that some day he would be released, since he was in truth innocent of any crime.

One night the snake came to the old man in his cell. The snake bit the man on his arm and then went away again. The old man's arm swelled up immediately from the effects of the snake's poison, and the pain became unbearable. "That snake has returned evil for good," mourned the old man to himself. "How absurd that is!"

But a little later, who should return to the old man's cell but the snake, holding a small glass bottle in his mouth. The snake applied the contents of the bottle to the painful swelling on the arm; at once the swelling subsided and the pain ceased, so that the old man was completely cured. Then the snake disappeared once more.

In the morning the old man heard a great commotion outside. He listened and discovered that the magistrate's wife had been bitten during the night by a snake and now seemed about to die from the poison. He guessed that it was the very same snake that had bitten him—the snake he had rescued from the flood. So he sent word to the magistrate that he knew how to cure the wife's injury. The magistrate sent for him immediately, and the old man took the rest of the magic ointment that the snake had brought to him. He applied it to the lady's wound, and at once she became completely well again. Thus the grateful snake repaid the old man for his kindness, as the deer had done.

Now the magistrate was convinced of the old man's innocence and had him released at once. As for the wicked foster-son, he was arrested in his turn, and punished for his ingratitude and evil ways.

*   *   *

"The Deer and the Snake" is an ancient Korean folk tale. It illustrates the contrast between the belief of simple people in the almost anthropomorphic characteristics of animals, and their friendship to man, especially to any human who befriends them, and the lack of filial piety or simple gratitude (a cherished Confucian precept) of a son towards his father.

Dojo-ji

The young and handsome priest Anchin used to come on pilgrimage from the monastery of Dojo temple to Kumano. At Kumano, it was his custom to spend the night at an inn at Masago. The proprietor of this inn had a charming little daughter named Kiyohime. Anchin used to play games with the little girl, and as the years went on and she grew to be a young lady, he was quite unaware that she was finding him attractive as a man and was falling in love with him.

On one of his visits, when Kiyohime had developed into a beautiful young woman, she revealed to Anchin the depth of her love for him—a sacrilegious love for a holy man that he, committed to his vows of celibacy, could not condone or return. So he spurned her advances, finally and definitely, and returned to his monastery with the determination never again to visit Masago. But the girl, distraught with love, turned to the intercession of evil divinities to aid her by means of magical powers. She even tried the traditional incantation and sorcery of punishment of unfaithful lovers called *ushi no toki mairi*. That is, she visited a temple at the Hour of the Ox (two hours past midnight), and there maltreated a straw effigy of Anchin.

Kiyohime had gone to a temple close by for this special incantation. She had dressed herself in white, the traditional color of mourning, balancing three burning candles in a metal tripod on her head, her hair hanging loose. A mirror hung on her breast, and in her left hand was the straw effigy of her lover; in her right hand she carried spikes and a hammer. Nailing the effigy to a tree outside the temple, she prayed to the gods for revenge. This unhappy pilgrimage was repeated three times, but all in vain. Anchin, ceaselessly moving his beads and repeating his prayers, sheltered himself from the girl within the safe walls of his monastery. In this he had the assistance of the chief abbot, to whom he had confided the whole unhappy story.

Finally, when Kiyohime, quite beside herself, came repeatedly to the monastery and demanded entrance, Anchin hid himself within the great new bronze bell of his temple, a huge bell, more than six feet in height, and so heavy that one hundred men could not budge it. The abbot gave instructions that no women were to be permitted to enter the precincts of the temple.

Kiyohime, her love now hardened into jealousy and hatred, arrived at the temple in disguise, claiming to be a girl named Hanako who was collecting funds to re-build a temple that had been destroyed by fire. To get alms for her cause, she begged to be allowed into the courtyard to see the new temple bell of Dojo and to perform a dance in its honor.

This permission was granted, and Kiyohime then performed a lengthy dance, during which she changed her costume several times (as a snake changes its skin). At the end of the dance, the young woman approached the bell and began to strike it with the magic hammer she carried. The strong ropes suspending the bell (as thick as those worn by a great Sumo wrestler) suddenly broke, and the bell crashed resoundingly to earth, im-prisoning beneath its weight the unfortunate Anchin. At that very moment, the face of Kiyohime changed into that of the sorceress Hannya, and her body into that of a huge snake, which wound its coils tightly about the bronze bell. Circling round and round the bell in ever tighter circles, the serpent caused the bell finally to be-come red hot. The serpent too emitted red flames from its mouth and the intense heat eventually melted the bell, which collapsed with a great roar. The priests of Dojo-ji watched in horror, unable to do anything except listen to the final prayers of the unfortunate monk, whose ashes they later removed from the debris.

As for Kiyohime, she disappeared forever from the world of men.

*   *   *

"Dojo-ji" is one of the most famous tales in the annals of Japanese literature. It is a classic tale, found in both the Kabuki and Noh theater repertories, and is read by all schoolchildren. It is the ancient tale of the vengeance of a woman scorned.

The guardian snake

One day a small boy named Feng-sheng went into the mountains to gather faggots for his mother. While he was searching about in the tall grass and underbrush, he came upon a very large egg. The boy was so pleased with this prize that he brought it home, where he hid it in a chest. A few days later, to his amazement, the shell of the egg broke and a tiny blue snake crawled out.

The little boy loved his new treasure very much indeed; and so he kept him in a special box. He tended him carefully, and soon the snake grew bigger. At first he was as thin as a noodle; gradually, he became as thick as a rope; and finally, he was a large, full-grown snake, as thick around as the handle of a stout hoe. Since Feng-sheng could no longer keep him tucked away in a box, he permitted him to move about freely on the ground.

The blue snake was extremely gentle, and never attempted to strike or bite anyone. One day, as he was playing happily in the garden, a flock of chickens came by and looked at him there, rolling about. Some of the chickens bit the snake. The surprised snake cried out for help. His little master came to his rescue promptly, drove off the chickens, and helped his pet back into the house. The snake was not badly hurt, but he was covered with small drops of blood.

A few days later, Feng-sheng heard the snake call out again. Rushing outside, the boy discovered a group of frogs, some of them attempting to eat his snake! Really angry this time, Feng-sheng caught the frogs, killed them, roasted them over a fire, and ate their legs. (This was the beginning of the delicious dish called frogs' legs!)

One night when Feng-sheng was sleeping soundly, a large rat jumped down from a ceiling rafter, bit the boy on the neck, and killed him. Next morning the blue snake discovered his small master dead. He was very, very sad, but then his sadness turned to implacable anger toward the rat that had robbed him of his master.

So from that moment on, the snake made the rat his special enemy. Every time he saw a rat, he killed him and ate him right down to and including the tail!

And ever since that long-ago time, blue snakes have always been covered with small dark spots, like blood, and they have always killed and eaten both chickens and rats, for they are still taking revenge for Feng-sheng and his pet. But they never harm a human being.

Even today, in old houses, there is always a snake to be found hiding somewhere in the roof to keep watch over the household, especially over small boys and their affairs. And even today, in China, people kill chickens to make sacrifice to the Snake God, which is called the Blue Dragon (*Ch'ing Lung*). And they humbly ask the blue dragon snake to permit no harm to befall them.

*   *   *

The ancient Chinese were fond of inventing tales—as indeed were all ancient peoples—perhaps partly to pass the time, partly to amuse children, often to create an account of some natural phenomenon. The tale "The Guardian Snake" can explain both the reason why snakes eat rodents and why certain snakes are spotted. It again reveals the friendship that can develop between animals and humans.

7 THE HORSE

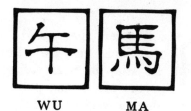

午　馬

WU　　　　MA

The Horse

All over the world, the horse is mentioned very early in man's history. In Asia, the horse, of a species known as the Mongolian pony, is generally a smaller variety than that in the West. In the Asian animal zodiac, the horse represents valor and endurance, and is classed with the fire element. In Buddhism, the horse is honored as one of the Seven Treasures.

In the Japanese Shinto tradition, the horse embodies the concept of ritual purification and serves the purpose of hearing the confessions of worshippers. In order to achieve purification of spirit, people were required to cleanse their minds of all evil, in both thought and deed; this was achieved by making confession of misdeeds, and for this purpose the horse was considered ideal because of his two long ears! So white horses were kept at Shinto shrines, and even today white horses bedecked with elegant trappings are paraded proudly at Shinto festivals. But within the shrines themselves, for lack of space, the horses came to be replaced by wooden tablets or by paintings of horses on wood. Such paintings, called *ema*, are still used, and some shrines boast large and valuable collections of *ema*, many the work of prominent artists.

In China the horse was considered precious medically, since many parts of his anatomy were used in making medicines. A treatise called *Ma Ching*(馬経), or *The Horse Classic*, written in the seventeenth century, describes the animal, noting his "thirty-two marks," of which the eye is the pearl, "round as a banner-bell"; the pupil is "bean-shaped, well-defined, with white striae"; the iris "has five colors (meaning) he will be long-lived"; his nose bears lines "like the characters *kung* and *hao*"; he will "live to see forty springs"; the forehead is described as "higher than the eyes"; the mane "soft, with ten thousand delicate hairs"; the face and chops "without flesh"; the ears "like a willow leaf"; the neck "like a phoenix's or cock's when crowing"; the mouth large and deep "with lips like a box close joining"; the incisors and molars "far apart"; the tongue "like a two-edged sword and of good color"; the gums "not black (meaning) he will have a long life"; the whole animal "lean as to flesh, fat as to bones," never starting at sounds or fearful of sights. A horse with his tail elevated is reckoned a good sign. The head is described as inclined and the neck as "crooked with three prominences on the crown"; the horse's sinews are "like the deer's"; the bones of the leg are small and the hooves light; the fetlocks are "in the shape of a bow"; the breast and shoulders are broad and project somewhat forward; the head is long and the loins short; the belly hanging and the hair on it growing upward; the hooves strong and solid; the knees high and the joints uniform; the flesh on the back is thick, making it "round as a wheel"; the scapula are "like a guitar"; the femur is inclined; and the tail "flows like a comet, the hairs all soft."

The Chinese thought of the horse as representing speed and perseverance; a quick-witted youth was often referred to as a "thousand-*li* colt." Many famous steeds were described in legends and used as art motifs. The sleeves of the robe of a Manchu official were shaped like a horse's hoof, and the queue worn by the Chinese during the Manchu dynasty was said to have been adopted in imitation of a horse's tail, since the animal was so highly valued.

The earliest reference to a horse in China is to the traditional *lung ma*, the "dragon horse," a mythical creature with the head of a dragon and the body of a horse. In Tibet, a similar animal was known as a "wind horse."

The horse's speed has caused him to be compared with the sun, which traverses the earth daily. So in legend, the sun is sometimes associated with the horse or with fiery steeds—as in the Greek legend of Apollo driving the chariot of the sun across the skies each twenty-four hours. And in early, primitive religions, horses were often sacrificed in worship of the sun. The seahorse too is a symbol of the sun, and the relationship of the sun and the sea is often equated with that of fire and water.

Lord Buddha is said to have had a famous white steed called Kantanka who, abandoned by his master when the mystic sought enlightenment, refused to eat, and neighed mournfully near the grove where his master sat in contemplation.

White horses have always been especially prized and their use sometimes restricted to royalty or to religion. Because the people of the Orient invested the horse with qualities of purity, nobility, and wisdom, it is natural that this animal should be held in wide esteem. Chinese men of letters who coached candidates for the Confucian examinations were called "horses"; the apartments where the examinations were held were known as "horse sheds"; and the students themselves were said, when taking the all-important examinations, to be "riding the horses."

Since the horse has traditionally held such an exalted position among men, is highly esteemed for his sensitivity, alertness, intelligence, and strength, and has always been a trusted companion and friend to man, it is generally good for a boy to be born in the Year of the Horse. Horse-year people are thought to be smooth-spoken, given to compliments, and generous of spirit; therefore they are popular. With their cheerfulness and alertness, they manage to accomplish a great deal; they make friends easily, and they handle their finances ably. Such people are often talented in many directions and clever in doing things with their hands. They tend to like dress and high style, but they are also prone to be impatient and may, if provoked, prove highly emotional. They are independent and can be quick to anger. But they like crowds, entertainment, and gaiety.

Even so, among the Japanese, the horse year has one sharp and decided limitation: it is considered to be not a good year at all for women! Indeed, so prevalent is the acceptance of this superstition that whenever this particular year comes around, the birth rate drops, for families fear the arrival of a daughter in that year! Tradition in Japan has it that such an unfortunate female will have a hard time ever getting married, for she will be stigmatized as willful, stubborn, even violent, capable of killing up to seven spouses (if she can first get them)! The very worst fate of all for a family is to have a daughter born in the Year of the Fiery Horse (sometimes called the Year of the White Horse) which comes around once every sixty years, at the time when the zodiac animal is the horse and the zodiac element in the ascendancy is fire. (The last such concatenation occurred in 1966.) Paradoxically, this year would be fantastically good for the birth of a male: he would be bound to be exceptional in many ways and to make an amazingly fine catch for some lucky girl. Perhaps in time the Women's Liberation Movement can reverse these current notions.

As far as marriage goes, people born in the horse year will have the happiest time of it if their mate has been born in the tiger, dog, or sheep year. Failing that, they can settle for someone from the years of the dragon, snake, monkey, cock, or boar. People from the ox, rabbit, and horse years are to be avoided as marriage partners. The most unlikely choice of all would be someone from the Year of the Rat!

The old horse knows the way

In the Period of the Warring States (according to the *Spring and Autumn Annals*), the kingdom of Shan-Yung invaded the Kingdom of Yen.

Because he was a friend of the King of Yen, the Prince of Chi dispatched his troops to assist the people of Yen and to rescue them from defeat. With this support, the combined forces of Yen and Chi were able to defeat the army of Shan-Yung and to put it to rout.

But the king of Shan-Yung was not prepared to give up. He requested military aid from his ally, the kingdom of Ku-Chu, so that he could seek revenge. This was given, but the soldiers of Ku-Chu were also routed by the defense of Yen and Chi. At this juncture, the king of Ku-Chu named one of his generals, Huang-hua, to proceed to the princely state of Chi, ostensibly to accept defeat and to offer to help the Prince of Chi capture the king of Ku-Chu. The Prince of Chi was quite taken in by this graceful gesture, and he permitted his soldiers to start off in his company, all of them under the general's leadership.

General Huang-hua then craftily led the soldiers of Chi into the desert of Han-hai, a barren wasteland where there was no grass or vegetation of any kind, no water for hundreds of *li*, and where no living thing moved about. To make matters worse, it was the very dead of winter. In the midst of the howling winds and drifting sands, the poor soldiers of Chi were distraught and on the point of freezing to death. By the time the Prince of Chi realized that something was gravely amiss, the deceitful general of Ku-Chu had slipped away and disappeared. Because night had fallen and the darkness only added to their plight, it was decided that the army of Chi would wait until morning to plan a strategy.

When dawn broke, the seriousness of the situation became clear. Many of the foot soldiers had died along the march or had perished during the freezing chill of the night. Those who remained realized only too well that if they could not quickly find their way out of this desert land, they too would starve or freeze to death. But how could they help themselves? Not one had ever before been in this terrain, nor could they reconstruct the circuitous route by which they had been brought here. The shifting sands had obliterated their tracks.

But there was among their number a famous elder statesman, the wise Kuan-chung, the prime minister of the princely state of Chi. He recalled the fact that, among all animals, horses have the finest, clearest, most marvelous memories for the roads they have traveled. In this capacity they were indeed said to excel human beings. So this elder statesman approached the Prince of Chi and said to him: "Sire, it is my belief that if we permit it, our noble steeds can lead us safely out of these dangers." The prince, with no alternative plan to suggest, gave his assent without hesitation. Whereupon the soldiers, instead of leading their horses, or guiding them in any way, dropped their reins as they were commanded, and followed their animals. Just as Minister Kuan anticipated, the horses were able to lead them all back along the route they had come until they were safely at home again in their own kingdom.

So it can be seen that a humble animal, even one that is old and worn out, still possesses his own virtues and his own strengths. In the case of the noble horse, this virtue and strength lies, in part at least, in the fact that he will always know the way back from wherever he has traveled.

And from this it can be appreciated that no living creature should ever be belittled, but rather that the best and highest use should be made of every thing and of every person on this earth, according to his individual gifts and abilities. For truly, wisdom lies in knowing how to use things and people to their highest potential.

* * *

"The Old Horse Knows the Way" is told as it was written in the Chinese classics. It is ascribed to Han Fei-tzu, a contemporary of Confucius.

 # How the horse got his lovely big teeth

In olden times, horses had only smallish lower teeth, and none at all in the tops of their mouths. Buffalo, on the other hand, had beautiful full sets of teeth, upper and lower.

One day it happened that Mr. Horse was invited to attend a special banquet, where he knew there was bound to be an excellent menu served. Wanting to make the very most of this opportunity to feast, the horse asked his friend the buffalo to lend him for the occasion his set of upper teeth, so that he could chew his food better and get more taste and pleasure from it.

Reacting like a good friend, the buffalo at once removed his upper teeth from his large mouth and gave them to Mr. Horse, who then went merrily off to his party, where his stomach was soon filled with the very tastiest dishes.

After the dinner party was over with, the horse returned to his home, happy and replete. However, he failed to return to his friend the buffalo the set of teeth he had borrowed. Not wanting to appear impatient or lacking in trust, the buffalo waited a very long time before timidly broaching to his friend the return of his lovely white teeth.

But, when asked to give back the teeth, the horse replied: "My friend, let's run a race to see who should keep those teeth. If you can run as fast as I, I'll certainly return your teeth to you at once."

Immediately the horse was off down the road like an arrow shot from a bow. The poor buffalo tried to match his pace, but it was totally impossible; his vast bulk permitted him only to waddle along as best he could, far, far behind.

And so that is why, to this very day, buffalo have only lower teeth in their mouths, whereas horses have huge upper teeth that protrude in a vast yellow grin when they pull their upper lips back! Those teeth were never intended for them, and are much too big for their mouths. As for the buffalo, he has to chew slowly and do his best to toughen his upper gums so that his lower teeth will not damage them.

*   *   *

Since the patient, lumbering gray water buffalo is such a common animal for draught labor throughout Southeast Asia it is natural that some legends of the area should include him. "How the Horse Got His Lovely Big Teeth" is a humorous explanation for both the protruding upper teeth of the horse and the near-absence of similar teeth in the water buffalo. This tale was told to me by my Vietnamese students.

8 THE RAM

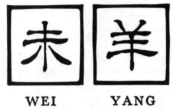

WEI   YANG

The Ram

The sheep or goat (called the hill-sheep) is the eighth symbolic animal of the twelve terrestrial branches, and the emblem of a retired life. The goat is one of the "six sacrificial animals" and was undoubtedly known in China long before the sheep was. (However, since the western variety of sheep is relatively uncommon in Asia, the goat or the deer, both better known there, are often used as the animal for the Year of the Ram. The characteristics of these three animals are somewhat mingled in fixing the qualities of the twelve-month ram year in the animal cycle.)

Since sheep, goats, and deer are all gregarious, moving about in flocks or herds, the year of the ram is expected to be marked by excellent cooperation among humans. Sheep dislike water, so care must be exercised against water accidents during this year. But the animals' strong foreheads and horns for butting indicate that the year's difficulties can be overcome through courage and fortitude. And, since the sheep is timid, defenseless, mild of nature, wanting little more than to be left alone to graze in the grass, it represents peace, and its year is thought to bode well for that scarce commodity. (The lamb of God, a symbol of Christianity, is well known.)

Animals as docile as deer, goats, and sheep are popular among the people, and a number of folk traditions have grown up around them. One is this: if a goat bleats with its head held high, it is surely going to rain! Another: when the goat brings forth kids, the farmer will have a bumper harvest. One of the most charming beliefs, springing from a concept of an early Chinese sage, is this: since lambs and kids, when suckling milk from their mothers, always take a respectful kneeling position, this is an expression of filial piety, and these animals therefore symbolize that great Confucian virtue.

According to an ancient Chinese legend, five venerable magicians, clothed in garments of five different colors and riding on rams of five different colors, met in Canton. Each of the rams bore in his mouth a stalk of grain that had six ears. These were then presented to the people of the district, to whom the magicians said: "May famine and dearth never visit your markets!"

Having uttered these words, the magicians immediately disappeared, and the rams upon which they were riding were changed into stone. From this old legend, Canton, the great city on the Pearl River in South China, came to be known thenceforth as the City of Rams.

In Korea during the Koryo dynasty (A.D. 918–1390), sacrificial rites for ancestors were thought to be incomplete without an offering of goat meat. Goats had been introduced from China to Korea during the early years of the Ming dynasty for use in such ancestor rites, so during that period Koreans came to believe that if they ate goat meat, they could commune more closely with the spirits of their deceased forefathers.

In the northern provinces of China and Korea, the domestic sheep was the broad-tailed species and was not so common as goats. In some parts of China where there were sheep, the long hair was shorn for use in garments. Because of the scarcity of good grazing, the animals were fed chiefly on cut fodder. The mutton was of high quality and was eaten chiefly by Muslims, the Chinese usually having small taste for it. A number of species of wild sheep have lived in the Altai and Daurian mountains in Mongolia, in Shansi, Hopeh, and Kansu Provinces. The wild sheep has a ram's head with long spiral horns and a deerlike body.

In Japan, because of the dampness of the climate, sheep are virtually unknown, so the goat is more commonly represented in art and has been substituted for sheep in tales brought from China. (The Chinese bred sheep in the dryer, colder northern area of their country, but in the southern part they too herded only goats.)

An interesting legend common to both countries concerns one of the eight "Old Men of the Mountains." This sage, called Huang Ch'u P'ing in China and Koshohei in Japan, decided when only fifteen years old that he wanted to go off in solitude to meditate in the mountains. But because he was then a goatherd, he had to take his charges with him. Alone in a cave he discovered in the hills, he meditated for forty years. At the end of that time, his brother, a priest, went into the mountains to look for him. He came finally to a region where the people told him about the hermit-goatherd dwelling in a nearby cave. The priest sought this spot out and, entering, he recognized his long-lost brother. But he saw no herd of goats. When asked about this, the sage showed his brother a large number of white stones lying about the floor of his cave. Raising his staff, he touched them. All were immediately transformed into living goats. "Here is my herd," he said.

The goat, like the sheep, is associated with peace on the basis of a homophone in which the Chinese ideograph for goat and that for *yang*, the masculine, positive principle of nature, have the same sound. The *yang*, the principle for good, is represented among the Eight Trigrams by three parallel horizontal lines ☰. So three goats are sometimes painted to symbolize a great threefold peace for the whole world.

In ancient days the Chinese foretold future events by reading cracks in the bones of roasted deer (as they did with the oracle bones of the tortoise). Deer heads were often used as offerings at shrines. The bones of deer, discovered in ancient shell mounds, are evidence that deer were abundant from earliest times. To the Chinese, the deer signified longevity. Chinese tradition claims that the deer lives to be at least twenty-five hundred years old. At the end of its first thousand years of life, its coat turns gray; after another thousand years, it becomes snow white; and finally, after still another five hundred years, its horns turn black, and this is the sign that the animal has achieved immortality! From that time on, it exists only on one special sacred fungus and crystal-clear mountain water. In this connection, a Chinese legend tells of a general and his army moving against a tribe of barbarian invaders. Suddenly they found themselves very much in need of water. At this point a white deer appeared, and the general thoughtlessly shot it. But instead of succumbing to the wound of the arrow that had pierced its body, the deer ran to a special spot, stood there a moment, then vanished completely. The astonished general found a bubbling well at the spot where the deer had stood.

There is a Chinese tradition that during the reign of the Yellow Emperor (Huang-ti)—around 3000 B.C.—deer were used as steeds and were ridden by barbarians coming to bring tribute to the court.

Many Chinese legends about the deer's immortality and special qualities are now thought to have been Taoist inventions to stop the hunting of wild deer and so prevent their extermination.

In Buddhism the deer is important because Gautama is believed to have been incarnated eleven times as a deer and to have delivered his first sermon in a deer reserve in the vicinity of Benares, now known as the Deer Park. In portrayals of that sermon, the "wheel of the law" is often represented between two deer.

Because of all these important associations, people born in the Year of the Ram are considered in many ways to be more fortunate than those born in other animal years. Such people are said to be tender-hearted and sympathetic, especially to those less fortunate than they. They are generous, loved by their friends, but are often taken advantage of because of their natural kindness and their timidity. They are generally unassertive—self-effacing, in fact; they spurn the struggle for power and leadership. They tend to be unsure of themselves, even to the point of speaking hesitantly. However, they are elegant, well-bred, and endowed with innate good taste. They are also talented and accomplished in the arts. Indeed, these wise and gentle people can live well on the fruits of their own talents. But they are passionate, pessimistic, often puzzled about life. Their passions are not only emotional, but are concerned with everything about which they feel keenly.

Ram-year people should, ideally, seek their marriage partners among those born in the rabbit, boar, or horse years. Next most suitable would be someone from the years of the tiger, dragon, snake, ram, monkey, or cock. Marriage should be avoided with anyone born in the years of the rat, ox, or dog.

The sheep is cousin to the ox

One fine day, God decided that He would destroy all the useless creatures of the world. "What in heaven's name is the use," He reasoned, "in keeping around so many creatures that are absolutely no good for anything?

Everyone should have a purpose. Really, I overdid myself in creation! Well, at least I can undo the unnecessaries." So did God reason unto Himself.

He decided, upon godlike reflection, that the ox could well be dispensed with—but then, upon further and deeper thought, He determined that that animal did serve a useful purpose in ploughing the fields. So He decided to spare the ox.

Then he turned His attention to the sheep. "You are a useless animal," said God to the sheep. "You never do a single thing except eat!"

But the sheep replied: "If you please, Sir, I live by my cousin's grace and favor, and I do not trouble men at all, my Lord."

So God asked the sheep: "Who is this cousin of yours?"

And the sheep replied: "The ox, my Lord."

"How can the ox be your cousin?" asked God. "I created everything, after all, and I was not aware that you had a cousin!"

The sheep answered him politely: "The ox's hooves are double, and so are mine. He has two horns and so have I, haven't I, my good Lord?"

Then God replied: "I agree that all this is as you say, but how then does it happen that you have a short tail, while the ox has a long one?"

"I get that from my mother's side, my Lord," replied the sheep.

*   *   *

"The Sheep Is Cousin to the Ox" is a small story, but one of the most charming to come from the Koreans.

How the deer lost his tail

Once upon a time, long ago, there were a little old woman and a little old man living together in a little old cottage at the edge of a big forest.

Every day they walked together in their garden, for they loved to see the new buds opening to greet them, and the little shoots peeping up through the ground to surprise them. They were gentle people, happy and contented. But, as they chatted together, the little old woman often said: "We have our cottage and our garden, and we are comfortable and happy here. But we do have one fear, alas. We do not fear the thunder, nor the lightning; we do not even fear the demons. But we do fear the Leo. The Leo is certainly our great fear."

And she rocked back and forth. But the little old man could never find out what she meant by the Leo.

Outside their door, the night was so dark that it seemed to enfold the cottage with a dark mantle. It was the dark of the moon and the animals were prowling cautiously about through the forest. As the old couple talked together they did not know that a tiger lurked outside their cottage door; neither did they know that a thief was hiding nearby in the darkness.

Crouched at the door, the tiger was listening to what the old man and the old woman were saying. When he heard the old woman say that they had one great fear, of the terrible Leo, he put one ear right up against the crack of the door to try to hear more about this creature. The tiger had never known fear himself. After all, was he not the great King of the Forest? He was not afraid of the jackals, he was not afraid of the foxes, he was not even afraid of the lion. But he had never seen a Leo, and the thought of this unknown creature made him uneasy. Yes, the tiger began to feel afraid.

Now all this time the thief had been hiding in the darkness, waiting to steal the old man's cow. He began to creep nearer and nearer to the house when, all of a sudden, the thief spied something moving in the darkness. This was when the tiger crouched to put his ear to the crack of the door. The thief saw the outline of an animal and thought it must surely be the old man's cow, which he had long wanted to steal. So he crept closer and put his hand out to seize it; but, instead of finding a cow, his hand touched the tiger. The thief was so frightened that he scrambled as fast as he could in the dark to the cottage roof to hide there from the tiger.

All this happened just as the tiger was listening at the cottage door and wondering what he would do if he saw a terrible Leo. At that very moment, through the denseness of the dark, he suddenly saw this strange figure scrambling to the roof, and the tiger thought to himself: "This must be the very Leo that the old couple so greatly fear. Who will save me now?" He crept softly around the house to try to escape from the fearful Leo.

Behind the house, at the edge of the forest, the frightened tiger met a deer.

He told the deer about the Leo, and how he had seen him climb to the cottage roof. The deer was very surprised and vastly relieved to find the fierce tiger so gentle and friendly, but when he heard about the mysterious

Leo, the poor little deer trembled all over in a panic. "Alas, who will save me from the terrible Leo?" he pleaded, with tears in his voice and in his big brown eyes.

Then the tiger pretended to be very fearless and wise. "Come with me, little deer, and I will take care of you; let us tie our tails together, so that we shall be able to help each other when we meet the Leo." The deer gladly consented, and he felt much safer after his tail had been tied to that of the strong tiger, so they crouched together close to the house.

Just then, a tree branch broke off and fell with a loud crack. The thief, hiding on the roof, was so frightened that he leaped from the roof edge, landing almost on top of the deer. The poor deer tried to escape into the forest, pulling his tail as hard as ever he could; but the tiger was pulling just as hard in the opposite direction.

Suddenly a dreadful thing happened! The little deer's tail broke right off!

The thief ran away. The tiger leaped into the forest in one direction, and the deer in another. But all that was left of the little deer's tail was a tiny tuft of fur. The rest of it was still tied into a knot at the end of the tiger's tail as he disappeared into the deep, dark woods.

And the dreadful Leo? No one ever saw *him*. The little old woman and the little old man put out the lamp and went off to bed and never knew all that had happened just outside their cottage door.

And this is exactly how the deer lost his tail.

*   *   *

"How the Deer Lost His Tail" is another Chinese story told by wandering entertainers.

The lamb lost on a branching road

The Period of the Warring States in Chinese history (*c.* 403–221 B.C.) happened also to be a time in which many famous scholars lived. There were many great sages then, among them Yang-chu, commonly known as Yang-tse. He was a contemporary of Mencius Meng-tse) and of Mo-tse. But Yang-tse expounded a theory of self-interest and of self-respect. His philosophy was the opposite of Mo-tse's altruistic universal love and of the concept of benevolence fostered by Meng-tse (the disciple of Confucius). Yang-tse thought one quite properly owed something to oneself.

Mencius criticized Yang-tse, in fact, saying that Yang-tse would not pull out one single hair to criticize the world. However, Yang-tse was really emphasizing the importance of self-esteem and self-interest in a wholly worthy sense.

So this fable, about the lamb lost on a branching road, comes from one of his writings—all of which were influenced by Lao-tse. Because Yang-tse's writings were lost, this is his story as retold by one of his contemporaries, Lieh-tse.

It seems that one day a neighbor of Yang-tse lost one of his sheep. So this neighbor sent out all his servants and relatives to search for the lost lamb, and went along himself to aid in the search. When he heard about this, Yang-tse was greatly surprised, and he said to the neighbor: "You have lost only one lamb. Why should you mobilize so many people to search for one animal?"

The neighbor answered: "It is because there are so many branching roads and byways in front of this house. We don't know which one this lost lamb might have taken. We must therefore assign at least one person to search along each path."

Yang-tse was kindhearted, and he sent his own servant out into the area to assist the neighbor in his search. After a fruitless day of seeking here and there, the servant returned. Yang-tse promptly asked him whether or not the lamb had been found. The servant responded in the negative.

Therefore Yang-tse was even more surprised. "How can so many men search and not be able to locate one sheep?" he asked.

His servant answered: "Not only are there many branch roads in front of that house, but each branch road in turn has many branches of its own. So we can never be sure what turns and twists the lamb took. And we must keep returning to seek further."

Yang-tse appeared now to be greatly disturbed and unhappy. He lapsed into silence and deep thought, refusing to speak. His disciples, seeing this, were worried and puzzled, so finally they roused him, saying: "Master, it is, after all, only a lamb that is lost, and that lamb is not even yours. So this is not an important matter to you. Why should you be so concerned about it?"

Yang-tse looked up at them and answered: "Alas, you don't understand me. What I am unhappy about is not the little lamb that is lost. I am really thinking about the branches in the road that caused the lamb to stray. So it is with our studies. When we follow them, if we lack concentration, if we don't have determination and direction, pursuing our studies with a clear objective, won't we be just like that little lamb that got lost in the branch routes? Won't we waste our time and our lives? In the matter of following out our study, therefore, we should not strive for too high a goal, or try to achieve too many things. If we do, we run the risk of getting lost, of going astray, just like that poor little lamb."

* * *

The Chinese story, "The Lamb Lost on a Branching Road," is a very old tale, supposedly the heritage of famous Chinese sages, and reminiscent of the Christian tale of Christ's love for one lost sheep.

9 THE MONKEY

SHEN   HOU

The Monkey

Asians know the monkey well. He's native to their part of the world, and they find him enormously amusing, as well as a legendary source of assistance in trouble, despite his natural bent for mischief. The monkey plays an important role in early Chinese myths of the creation, and on the basis of this the Asians believe that the monkey has supernatural powers. Like some of the other special animals, they believe, he lives a very long time indeed—as long, in fact, as four thousand years, at the end of which he is metamorphosed into an old man!

Because some kinds of monkeys form long tail-chains to swing across chasms and rivers, the Japanese and Chinese have taken to calling man-made spans "monkey bridges." Monkeys are thought, too, to have a special affinity for the moon, especially for the new moon, which they greet with chitterings of delight. At the time of the waning moon, monkeys are observed to feel depressed, and when there is a lunar eclipse, they become positively disturbed! Many Asian paintings show the monkey reaching upward toward the moon, or downward as if to snatch the moon's reflection from the waters. A well-known Zen poem reads:

> *A pair of monkeys are reaching*
> *For the moon in the water*

Buddhists sometimes reveal an ambivalence toward the monkey, for while they venerate him on the one hand for having (according to legend) accompanied the famous priest Yuan Chuang (or Hsuan Tsang) to India to help him obtain and bring back to China the true texts of the Buddha's teachings, on the other hand they view him (because of this apparent snatching at the moon) as a symbol of greed. So they classify the monkey as one of the "Three Senseless Creatures": the tiger, who is always angry; the deer, who is always lovesick; and the monkey, who is always greedy and grasping (a folly for which he pays a high price if he reaches too far for the moon's reflection and is drowned).

The Japanese, in fact, have a fable entitled "The Monkey Seizes the Moon," which is a variant of Aesop's fable about the dog who tried to catch the shadow of his bone in a brook. This Japanese fable is in reality a Buddhist parable about overreaching oneself; it concerns some long-armed monkeys who, seeing the moon's reflection in a well under a tall tree, resolved to catch it. They made a long chain of themselves from the tree to the water, but the branch from which they swung suddenly broke, and so they were drowned.

Probably the greatest of the Chinese monkey stories is the famous "Journey to the Western

Paradise," written in the sixteenth century by Wu Ch'eng-en. It concerns the myriad adventures of a fabulous and supernatural monkey of amazing strength, charm, and versatility. His feats are incorporated into a whole cycle of legends that includes that of the famous seventh-century trip to India by the Buddhist priest to fetch back the sacred scriptures. Accompanying the priest and the monkey were also a white horse and a sacred pig. As the result of this successful expedition, in which Monkey performed amazing feats in leading the way and rescuing his companions from danger, Monkey was rewarded by achieving Buddhahood himself, becoming thereby a rather unorthodox saint, somewhat subdued by the mild influence of Buddhism but with that mischievous nature still very apparent.

The Japanese retain the monkey in the Buddhist legends from China and include him in their indigenous tales. To start with, one of their own important Shinto deities, Okuninushi, the original deity of Izumo (who surrendered his throne to the imperial ancestors when they came down from heaven to rule Japan) had a monkey serving him as attendant and messenger. So at shrines honoring Okuninushi, the stone gate guardians are replaced by seated stone monkeys wearing bibs, and monkey figures are found inside these shrines.

And of course there is the famous Japanese story of the "See No Evil; Hear No Evil; Speak No Evil" monkeys, carved on a stable at the Nikko shrines.

One of the oldest and most popular of the Japanese fairy tales, "Momotaro," or "Peach Boy," has the young hero accompanied by a monkey, a dog, and a pheasant when he goes off in quest of treasure.

But the chief home of the monkey cult is probably India, where, from time immemorial, the monkey has been revered for what is believed to be his magic power. He has been fed, protected, and allowed to roam at will, becoming thereby quite a nuisance (although few Indians would admit this aspect of the animal). Indian interest in the monkey is concentrated in the exploits of the monkey god Hanuman, son of the wind god Vayu and possessed of tremendous superhuman power. Hanuman could assume any shape or size, could fly through the air to infinity in a moment, could leap through space, pluck a mountain as one might a flower, turn a somersault of six thousand miles. In addition to all this prowess, he possessed infinite wisdom. He it was who found Sita, the beloved wife, for Prince Rama (in the great Hindu epic the *Ramayana*) and was rewarded by the promise of life on earth "as long as men exist."

So people born in the monkey year are usually pleased with their year. They are declared to be clever and skillful people, especially in large-scale operations; they are passionate, strongly inventive, and original. They can solve difficult problems with great ease and are adroit in managing their financial affairs. They have outstanding memories, store up vast quantities of knowledge, are curious and observant. Their weakness lies in their tendency to be erratic, to lack constancy, and to be somewhat contemptuous of others, so that they will, for one example, sometimes agree with others only in order to be expedient. But, although prone to weakness in the area of human relationships (because of their own impatience), monkey-year people are greatly valued for their skills and cleverness. They can be successful at whatever they choose to do in life, but they must guard against becoming easily discouraged and then wanting to abandon a project. They must also guard against alienating people by talking too much!

Monkey-year people marry best with someone from the rat or dragon years. They should be wary of mating with someone from the snake or boar years. The worst marriage possible for them would be with someone from the tiger year. If a rat-year or a boar-year person is not available or appealing, then someone from the ram year or the dog year will do.

 # The monkeys and the chestnuts

Long ago, during the Sung Dynasty (A.D. 960–1279), there lived a man called Tzu-kung. As it happened, this Tzu-kung was extremely fond of animals, all animals— but especially so of monkeys. And so he kept many monkeys in the garden of his home and attended with great care to their daily needs. In this way, Tzu-kung came to learn a great deal about the monkey character and personality, and he understood them well.

In their own turn, the monkeys in his garden were very fond of Tzu-kung, and they paid such careful attention to him that they came to understand the words he spoke. All this close association and comradeship created a good deal of mutual affection, and so, before many years, Tzu-kung found himself raising a very large number of monkeys indeed.

Unfortunately, it was about this time that Tzu-kung's business affairs began to go badly. Soon it became increasingly difficult for him to feed such a large flock of animals. Reluctantly, he came to the conclusion that he really must reduce the amount of food he was giving the monkeys daily. But Tzu-kung knew very well that monkeys have extremely bad tempers when hey become upset; he realized that if he reduced their food allowance without explaining the reason to them very clearly and very carefully, they were sure to become exceedingly angry and overwrought, and this would create chaos instead of serenity in his garden.

So Tzu-kung determined to talk the whole matter over with his monkeys in the frankest possible way. He called all the animals together and explained the situation.

"Well now," he said, "I can no longer afford to give you the same amount of food I've been serving you, since my business affairs are now in bad shape, and so I just don't have the money to buy things freely at the market. As you know, I have always served each of you four chestnuts in the morning and four chestnuts in the evening. But from now on, I shall have to give you each *three* chestnuts in the morning and four chestnuts in the evening. I hope you will appreciate my position and offer me your understanding."

Alas! When the monkeys heard that their master was about to reduce their daily intake of food, they did indeed become excessively excited and upset. They chattered wildly, pulling back their lips and exposing their strong teeth in really hideous expressions. And they shrieked and jumped angrily all over the garden.

Tzu-kung became somewhat alarmed at this display of violent emotion, and so he immediately offered them a compromise:

"Well, then, I've decided to increase the size of your morning meal! I'll give you four chestnuts in the morning and three chestnuts at night!"

As soon as the monkeys heard their master declare that their breakfast allowance would be increased, they became extremely happy.

"Why, this is very nice," they said. "Our master is not cutting down on our food after all!"

And they immediately quieted down and were well satisfied with what they considered their victory. And peace and serenity reigned once more in the garden of the wise Tzu-kung!

* * *

The tale "The Monkeys and the Chestnuts" is a telling comment on human, as well as animal, foibles. It is an ancient Chinese classical story, attributed to the great sage Chuang-tse.

A monkey returns a kindness

A very long time ago, in a fishing village on the southern island of Kyushu, there lived happily together an honest, hardworking fisherman, his wife, and their small baby son.

One day when the tide was out, the wife put her baby on her back and went out with her neighbors to gather shells on the beach. It happened to be very fine weather that day, so the beach was crowded with villagers, all seeking the best shells.

To make her task easier, the fisherman's wife took her baby from her back, laid him in his blanket on a large rock, and asked a neighbor's son to keep his eye on him. Then, free of this responsibility, she set busily to work.

While she was picking up shells, she noticed a monkey playing on the beach at a little distance from the villagers. It appeared that he had come down from a nearby mountain.

"Look at that monkey over there," said the fisherman's wife to one of her neighbors. "I wonder what he can be up to? Let's go have a look."

So the two women approached the animal. Oddly, he did not flee at their approach. He moved back and forth restlessly, but remained where he was. To the women it seemed that the animal was trapped in some way and could not free himself. "So strange," said one woman to the other. "There must be something the matter with him."

By this time they had got close enough to the monkey to note that his paw was caught in a large shell.

"Oh, now I understand," said the fisherman's wife. "He must have been trying to pull the meat from the shell when it snapped shut on his paw." In truth, the monkey was struggling desperately to jerk his paw from the trap, while the shell was trying to bury itself even deeper in the sand. It was an amazing sight. One of the people who had gathered to watch picked up a huge rock to kill the monkey with; she hated these animals, for they frequently despoiled farms.

But the fisherman's wife took pity on the trapped beast and asked that his life be spared. While all this was going on, the ocean tide had started to come in, and huge waves were beginning to dash on the shore. The poor monkey was in real trouble, rolling about on the sand, struggling with the shell, and now getting splashed by the water. Many of the shell gatherers had given up and gone home.

But the kindhearted wife forced open the shell and set the monkey's paw free. Pitying the shell, too, she buried it gently in the wet sand.

To the monkey she said: "Let me warn you not to rob our farms any more." And the animal appeared to comprehend what she was saying to him. And yet, in the next instant, and before the poor woman could do a thing to stop him, the monkey leaped to the rock on which her baby was lying, snatched him up, blanket and all, and ran away with him toward the mountain.

The mother was astonished at this act of ingratitude. Angrily, she cried out to the monkey that he was returning evil for good, all the time running after him to get her baby back. Those of her neighbors who were still around ran along with her, reminding her that she should never have spared the animal's life.

Even with the baby under his arm, the monkey ran so fast that no one could catch up to him. While the mother screamed that he must return her baby, the beast finally climbed a tall tree, crouching on a top branch, the baby still clutched to him, as the mother and her friends gathered on the ground at the bottom of the tree. They could do nothing, so one neighbor volunteered to run back to the village and fetch the baby's father to the scene.

Meantime the monkey, with the baby in his right arm, began to sway with his left arm the branch on which he was perched. The baby became disturbed at this unexpected sensation and started crying loudly. The mother, helpless at the bottom of the tree, realized the danger of her child, and felt as if her heart would break.

At this juncture a huge eagle suddenly came swooping down from the mountain beyond. Now everyone feared that the eagle would snatch the baby from the monkey and carry him off to eat him. The child's mother closed her eyes and prayed earnestly to Lord Buddha for his help.

As the eagle dove down upon the monkey and his prize, the monkey suddenly released his left arm, causing the branch he was shaking to react like a bow drawn to the full. The branch snapped back with such force that, striking the eagle's head, it killed him instantly! The huge bird dropped head first to the ground. Again the monkey seized the branch, for a second eagle was now swooping upon him. The wise monkey counterattacked at the right moment, knocking it down, too. In quick succession, five eagles were knocked dead to the ground in this fashion, while the villagers gazed fascinated at this strange battle. They understood that, while the monkey had been struggling with the shell on the beach, he had observed the eagles circling above, waiting for a chance to snatch the baby from the rock. As soon as he was released, therefore, he had repaid the benefactor's kindness by protecting her baby from the eagles.

Once the battle was ended and the danger gone, the

monkey came swiftly down from the tree and laid the baby gently at his mother's feet. Then he went back up the tree. By the time the child's father arrived, everything was settled, and the villagers rejoiced together as they returned home.

The fisherman later obtained considerable money by selling the beautiful wings of the dead eagles to a well-to-do merchant in a nearby town.

*   *   *

"A Monkey Returns a Kindness" is a very old Japanese legend, going back to the classics. This version has come down from the *Konjaku Monogatari*, vol. 29.

 # The priest and the monkey deity

Long, long ago there was a young Buddhist priest who went about the countryside with his begging bowl, wearing his brown robe, wide-brimmed straw hat, and sandals. While making his way about the country, he came to the province of Hida (now Gifu Prefecture), which is in a mountainous area. Following paths across the mountains, the priest became lost and did not know how to return to the world of human habitations. But, since there was really nothing else to do, he continued wandering about until finally he found himself at the foot of a large waterfall, so high that it appeared impossible to ascend the cliff it tumbled over. So he prayed to Lord Buddha for guidance and help, and just at that moment he heard footsteps behind him. Looking around, he perceived an old man wearing a large hat approaching him. Delighted at the sight of another human being, the priest immediately asked the way to the nearest village. To his surprise, he received no reply at all. Stepping down to the edge of the pool at the foot of the waterfall, the old man cast himself in. The priest was amazed at this act and decided that the old man must be an evil spirit of some sort. But, since he himself was helpless in the mountainous jungle, and he had decided that he preferred suicide to destruction by wild animals, he leaped into the waters, praying for peace after death.

But the cold water brought him back to sharp consciousness. He saw a shore nearby, and, crawling out of the water onto it, he realized that he had passed under the screen of the waterfall. To one side, he saw a road running straight ahead. He continued along this road, and in a very short time he found himself in a village. A man was running toward him, and as he drew near the priest could see that this was the same old man who had plunged into the mountain pool ahead of him. He was accompanied by another old man, dressed in a ceremonial yellow kimono. They beckoned the priest to accompany them, but, as he started to walk off with them, a number of the villagers emerged from their houses and tried to pull the priest in with them.

"Stop the violence!" cried the man in the yellow kimono. Then he suggested, "Why not let the village schoolmaster decide who should welcome this priest?" Since no one took exception to this, the priest was led off to the schoolmaster's house.

The schoolmaster appeared to be more than one hundred years old. "What is all this? What is going on?" he enquired.

"Sir, this is the priest that I found in the Land of the Rising Sun," answered the old man.

"Are you sure?" countered the schoolmaster.

"Positively certain," came the reply.

"Then he is yours."

And so the priest found himself being led away to the house belonging to the old man.

"I am no longer in the Land of the Rising Sun, then?" he demanded.

"Don't worry. You are in Paradise now, and can live happily here."

By this time they had reached the house of the old man. It was much larger than that of the schoolmaster, and all the family came out to greet the priest, who was shown into the best room. From then on, the priest found nothing but the most polite and hospitable attention shown him. Finally, one day the host asked the priest if he would consent to marrying his beautiful daughter.

The poor priest was amazed and startled at the suggestion, for he knew that priests were expected not to wed. At the same time, he felt that, should he refuse, some member of this strange family in this unusual world might kill him. So, asking the Great Buddha to forgive him for sinning, he married the young lady and entered upon the happiest time of his life. His wife seemed to take special pleasure in feeding him enormous repasts daily. He ate them and enjoyed them, but inevitably he began to put on weight; as he grew fatter, his wife seemed to become sadder. Often her husband found her weeping. But though he tried his best to discover the reason, he could not. One day he overheard a strange conversation between his father-in-law and a caller.

"You have found a nice husband for your daughter, and just in the nick of time. Now she will be safe."

"Oh yes," replied the master of the house. "Without him we would be doomed to great sadness next year."

The priest could not get this conversation out of his mind, and, insisting that his wife tell him the truth, he finally discovered the whole story. He was due to be devoured shortly by the village deity. His wife had been scheduled as the victim herself, but her father had found her a husband to substitute for her. She was fattening him because the deities were furious if they were offered thin victims, and, as vengeance, they then devastated all the village farmland. So the villagers had continued to offer a fat sacrifice annually.

The priest decided to kill the evil spirits. When the day finally came for him to be led to the spot of sacrifice, a nearly shrine, he managed to hide a short sword and prepared to do battle with the man-eating deity.

Before long, the door of the Ichi-no-kura, the shrine treasury, creaked open and many monkeys appeared. They were followed in turn by a huge monkey who acted sluggish as he turned toward his victim and prepared to devour him. But the priest raised himself quickly, struck down the large monkey with his dagger, and fastened him to a nearby tree. All the little monkeys ran away to the tops of trees in the area.

"I am going to kill you for all the crimes you have committed!" And the priest raised his sword to pierce the large monkey, who squealed and begged for mercy. Even the little monkeys descended their trees to apologize, but the intended victim tied them all up to tree trunks. Then he set the shrine ablaze. Seeing the fire from a distance, the villagers approached, and, realizing what had transpired, they agreed that this priest-husband was stronger than any deity they had ever heard of! He explained to the people that their tutelary deity who had frightened them so badly was nothing but a huge monkey. He ordered them to abandon such foolish practices as offering human sacrifices, and he beat the monkeys, then released them. They fled into the night.

The priest was immediately made village headman and ever afterward he lived a contented life with his wife. Everyone in the area of Hida knows of this tale, but no one knows the precise spot at which these strange events occurred.

*   *   *

"The Priest and the Monkey Deity" is another Japanese classic tale taken from the *Konjaku Monogatari*.

10 THE COCK

YU   CHI

The Cock

The cock is of celestial origin. At the very beginning of things, he was sent down by the Creator to ascertain what the world looked like. But he tarried so long (since he was well pleased with what he saw) that he was forbidden to return to heaven. That, at least, is an ancient Ainu myth.

The cock appears very early indeed in Japanese mythology. It plays a leading role in the Shinto sun myth. According to the *Kojiki* account, when the sun goddess Amaterasu Omikami retired to a cave in protest to the violence of her brother, Susano-o, thereby leaving the world in darkness, the cock was brought before the sealed cave to crow. This made the reluctant goddess think that the day had dawned without her presence. Her curiosity to determine if this could be possible led her to emerge from her hiding place, and the world was bright again. So, from that time forward, the cock has been considered the messenger of the sun goddess; at the Grand Shrine of Ise, devoted to the divine ancestors of Japan, gorgeously plumed, long-tailed species of cock are always to be seen around the shrines. The *torii* (gate) at the entrance to every Shinto shrine is in fact a replica of the cock's perch.

The image of a cock perched upon a large drum is also seen frequently in Asia. This alludes to an ancient Chinese legend recounting the story of the drum placed in early times before the emperor's palace to summon the troops in case of attack. But during the reign of the Emperor Yao, the times were so peaceful that the drum was not needed at all; consequently, the neighborhood fowl nested in it. In this manner the drum and the cock together became a symbol of peace in the land.

Another Chinese tale concerns an exploit of a son of Emperor Yao, the heroic Prince Tan Cho. Imprisoned on one occasion in the town of Kan Kok Kan, where the prison gates were always locked from sunset until cockcrow, the prince managed to escape in the night with his retainer Keimei, because the servant gave such a skillful imitation of the cock that the guards awakened and opened the heavy doors without question!

Another Chinese legend concerning the cock tells of one of the three women immortals, Ma Ku, who fled from her home, became a hermit in the mountains, and later ascended into heaven on the back of a large bird. This transpired because her cruel father threatened her for having taken pity on his overworked laborers. It had been his custom to permit them to stop their work only when the cock crowed at daybreak. In order to permit the workers some rest at an earlier hour, the daughter imitated the cock's crowing.

The cock is believed to embody the element *yang*, representing universal warmth, strength, and life. He is also thought to have the power of changing himself into human form to inflict good or evil upon mankind. The Chinese ascribe special virtues to the cock: the crown of his head is said to be the mark of his literary spirit; the spurs on his feet are tokens of a warlike disposition; and he is also a symbol of courage, since he fights his enemies bravely. (Cockfights are extremely popular throughout Asia.) At the same time, he is benevolent, always clucking for the hen to come and share when he scratches up grain. And he is faithful, for he never forgets the hour to crow. Additionally, he is a symbol of protection against fire, so a picture of a red cock is often pasted on the wall of a house for that reason.

Because ghosts disappear at sunrise, it is believed that the cock drives them away with his crowing. So a white cock is sometimes placed on the coffin in funeral processions to clear the road of demons. The Chinese claim that one of the three spirits of the dead comes into the cock when he meets the corpse, and in this fashion the spirit of the departed one is lured back into the house.

It was formerly customary for a bride and bridegroom to eat white sugar cocks during a wedding ceremony, as a protection against evil influences.

The bucolic pleasures of life in the country are depicted in designs showing a cock and a hen in a garden of rocks and peonies. A fowl on the roof is considered a bad omen, and it is extremely unlucky if it thunders while a hen is sitting on eggs!

People born in the Year of the Cock are considered to be profound thinkers, always busy and devoted to their work. Their tendency is to undertake more than they can accomplish, and then to be disappointed and frustrated when they can't achieve their goals. They are always sure they are right, and they want to be left alone to do things in their own way. So they tend to distrust others; as a consequence, their relationships with other people often suffer. Although they seem on the surface to be rather adventurous spirits, there is always a certain insecurity deep within themselves. They have selfish characteristics, and they are usually blunt and outspoken— another facet of their personality that tends to put people off. Cock-year people are not a whit shy, and, when the occasion calls for courage, they can reveal real bravery. Other people usually find them exceedingly interesting, if a bit difficult. The material fortunes of people born in the year of the cock are varied—sometimes good, sometimes bad. Because such people are not farsighted in financial matters, they tend to be improvident.

Cock-year people are happiest if married to ox-, snake-, or dragon-year mates. Second choice for them would fall upon someone from the years of the tiger, horse, sheep, monkey, or boar. People from the rat, cock, or dog years will make poor matches for anyone from the cock year. But the very worst match of all would be with somebody from the Year of the Hare.

Why does the cock eat the millipede?

Long ago the cock had a pair of beautiful horns on his head. But at that time there was a dragon who was prevented from ascending into heaven because he lacked a pair of horns. And so he offered the millipede as guarantor, and borrowed the horns from the cock!

When the millipede came for the horns, he said to the cock: "When you want your horns back, you must call out at dawn: 'Give me back my horns!' and they will be returned to you at once. You need have no occasion to be concerned in the least."

The kind cock knew how difficult it was to ascend to heaven, so, reassured by the good security the millipede offered, he loaned his horns without any hesitation, just twisting them right off his head. He also thought to himself that when the dragon returned from his visit to heaven, they could sit down and have a good conversation; he would ask the dragon to tell him how things were in heaven, and if it really was very beautiful there, as he had always heard. If it was true, he might consider going there himself some day, he thought.

So next morning at daybreak (for the dragon's visit was scheduled to be brief), the cock called out loudly: "Give me back my horns!" But, even though he repeated this demand ten times over, there was no sign at all of either the dragon or the horns. Worried, the cock promptly went off to complain to the millipede, who soothed him, saying: "If the dragon has not returned the horns this morning, then he will certainly do so tomorrow. At the very latest, the day after that. Just learn to be a little patient and your horns will soon be back on your head, just as before."

The cock did wait several days, but although he called out every morning at sunrise: "Give me back my horns!" they never did reappear. The cock was extremely annoyed at this deception and loss, as you can well imagine; therefore he ordered all the members of his family to eat the millipede at sight. Even so, the cock has not yet given up hope of getting his horns returned. He ordered his descendants always to call out at break of day: "Give me back my horns!" He still hopes that the dragon may hear him!

*   *   *

"Why Does the Cock Eat the Millipede?" is a Chinese tale that is repeated in varying versions. The millipede is a small, crawling, many-legged insect, somewhat like the centipede.

How the rooster lost his horns

Everyone knows that at sunrise each morning the rooster cries out shrilly: "*Lung-k'o-k'o-huan-huan-wo*," or, as some people repeat it: "Cock-a-doodle-doo." And a moment or so later, the hen replies: "*K'o-k'o-k'o-k'o*," or "Cluck-cluck-cluck-cluck."

But why do the rooster and the hen make these special sounds? This will tell you how an old Chinese tale explains it.

Long, long ago, the rooster had a beautiful pair of long horns growing out of his head. They made him look exceedingly tall and elegant. But his good friend the dragon had no horns at all, so *his* appearance, while impressive (especially when he was breathing fire from his nostrils) was yet, in all honesty, rather plain.

Now it so happened that one spring the Lord of Heaven decided to appoint a God of Rain to administer rainfall affairs and to control the distribution of rains over the entire earth. So he announced that such an appointment was pending, and asked all earthly creatures interested to make application for the job—a job both pleasant and remunerative, and one which carried rather high status as well. All interested parties were to submit their applications and qualifications to the Lord of Heaven himself; he, in turn, would have a personal interview with the applicant, investigate all claims, and subsequently announce his choice for appointment to this important new post in the heavenly hierarchy.

The first to apply for the job was the fox. The God of Heaven investigated the fox's credentials, but then declared that, in his opinion, the fox was too cunning and sly. He was rejected for the post.

Next to make application was the lion. Everyone thought he would stand an excellent chance. But no, the Lord of Heaven decided that the lion was too fierce.

Then the elephant went to post his application. Alas! The Lord of Heaven said that the elephant was far too clumsy for the job.

And so it went. Application after application was filed and rejected. Six months passed, yet no one satisfactory had been found to fill the vacant post as God of Rain.

Finally the rooster and the dragon heard about the search. The rooster thought that he might as well apply. But then, when he heard that animals as clever and cunning as the fox, as strong and fierce as the lion, as polite and ponderous as the elephant had all been refused and turned away, he was certain that he would never have a chance. "After all, I am small, I have nothing special to offer," thought he to himself. "How could I ever be considered seriously for such a responsible job?" And so he decided not to apply, after all.

When the dragon heard of the opportunity, he decided he'd certainly apply. "After all," he thought, "I'm a gay and active fellow. I'm reasonably honest, and not so cunning or sly as the fox. I'm very kind and considerate, not nearly so proud and fierce as the lion. I'm sinuous and fast-moving, not nearly so awkward and clumsy as the elephant. Why wouldn't I stand an excellent chance of being appointed?"

But he continued to ponder the matter. "The only thing that bothers me is that I'm a bit plain. Not really ugly, mind you, but, to be honest, I'm not so handsome as the rooster. Maybe that's because of my not having horns. Why don't I have beautiful horns like the rooster?"

So the dragon thought: "Why don't I ask to borrow the rooster's horns just for this special occasion?"

Early next morning, therefore, when the rooster was strutting about, taking his before-breakfast constitutional, the dragon approached him and said: "Good morning, Brother Rooster. How are you this fine morning?"

The rooster replied: "Good morning, Brother Dragon." And the two friends fell into conversation.

The dragon said to the rooster:

"Brother Rooster, did you happen to know that the Lord of Heaven is looking for a rain god?"

The rooster replied:

"Yes, as a matter of fact I had heard about that. But an ordinary, incompetent individual like me would never be selected for such a job, so why should I waste my time to go there and apply for it?"

"I understand what you mean, Brother Rooster," said the dragon. "But all the same, I'm interested in applying. And before I do, I'd like to borrow something from you just for this one important occasion. I wonder if it's possible?"

"Brother Dragon," answered the rooster, "we are good friends. Please tell me what it is that you want."

"If I could have your horns, they would add so much dignity to my appearance that I do believe I might stand a very good chance of being chosen," said the dragon, rather tentatively.

"Oh, so it's my horns that you'd like to borrow! I agree that they certainly would add a great deal to your appearance." But the rooster was a bit hesitant. He added: "If you borrow my horns, *you'll* look distinguished, but what about *me*? I'll be left very plain—even ugly!"

"Now, Brother Rooster, don't you worry your head about that! After all, this is just a temporary arrangement. Of course I'll return the horns to you promptly after the interview is over."

So, with this understanding, the rooster agreed to let the dragon have the use of his precious horns for the period of the job application. The dragon was simply delighted, as you can well imagine, and when the rooster had reluctantly unscrewed them from his head, the dragon happily put on the horns over his eyebrows, and went off for the appointment.

As he departed, the rooster said: "Good luck to you, Brother Dragon. Do take the best possible care of my horns, now, and bring them right back to me. I feel awfully naked."

"Don't you worry about a thing, Brother Rooster," said the dragon, preening this way and that. "Don't you worry a bit."

And the dragon did indeed successfully pass the interview and secure the appointment. He became the new God of Rain and, immediately after his induction into office, took complete charge of the rainfall all over the entire world.

But he forgot all about returning the horns to the rooster! Later, when the dragon came back home to visit, he saw the rooster and his family. But the dragon was quite swollen with the importance of his new post, and he never mentioned the borrowed adornment.

As for the rooster himself, he was many times on the point of asking for his horns back; but he always reflected that the dragon was, after all, his old friend, and he would not risk injuring their long-standing friendship even to get back the horns he loved so much.

But the rooster's wife, Mrs. Hen, was greatly disturbed when she noticed that her husband made no move to regain his lost property. She kept muttering: "*K'o-k'o-k'o-k'o*" as she went about her housework. Since *k'o* is the Chinese word for "horn," this was her subtle method of reminding her spouse to ask for his horns.

But poor Brother Rooster would have been too embarrassed to do that, and he never did ask for them. However, when the dragon departed, dragging his scales behind him, the rooster did call out: "*Lung-k'o-k'o-k'o-huan-huan-wo*! *Lung-k'o-k'o-k'o-huan-huan-wo*!" This meant: "Brother Dragon, please return my horns to me! Brother Dragon, please return my horns to me!"

The dragon did not take one bit of notice of this reminder, if indeed he even heard it, for he was making a great noise and clatter himself, clashing his scales and breathing out streams of fire and smoke. He was very filled with his self-importance, and he went directly back to heaven, where he had a large and imposing office befitting his new rank and style.

The rooster never got his horns back, and ever since then he has had to make do with the bright red comb that was left on top of his head when he unscrewed his horns. But every morning, from then until today, the rooster stretches his neck as far as he can, looks up to heaven, and cries out:

"*Lung-k'o-k'o-k'o-huan-huan-wo*! *Lung-k'o-k'o-k'o-huan-huan-wo*!*"

And Mother Hen follows him, muttering: "*K'o-k'o-k'o-k'o-k'o*! *K'o-k'o-k'o-k'o-k'o*!*"

But the dragon up in his heavenly office goes right on doling out the rains and paying no attention. Beside his desk he has a shining full-length mirror, and every now and then he looks into it, and preens.

* * *

The legend of "How the Rooster Lost His Horns" comes from the Chinese classics.

How the cock got his red crown

Far in the west of China, the Miao tribespeople of the high mountain area watch the sun sink behind the rugged mountains of Tibet, and, as the shadows lengthen across their courtyards, they gather to hear the village storyteller relate again the legends of their tribes.

Long, long ago, when the world had just been made, this great land had six suns, rather than just one sun, shining up in the sky! But one spring, after the farmers had put in hard weeks of sowing crops, the rains refused to come at their appointed time, so that the constant blazing of the six big suns dried up every tender shoot.

Now at this time the great Emperor Yao ruled China. When he saw this natural disaster that was so afflicting his people, he became very sad. To his courtiers he said: "If those six suns continue shining like this, my people will all surely die." But no one could do anything about it at all. And so, day after day, the six suns rose in the heavens and burned up all the crops.

Then the ten wise elders of the village gathered to discuss what could be done. At length one old man said: "The only way is to shoot the suns and kill them."

When Emperor Yao heard this, he was greatly moved, and he sent his couriers far and wide to select the best archers in the kingdom and summon them to court.

Each of these archers was, of course, exceedingly strong. Each carried his great bow slung over his shoulder as he came proudly to serve the great emperor.

The people of the village and the ten wise old men gathered under the burning skies to watch the archers test their skill. As soon as Emperor Yao appeared, they let loose their arrows. But alas, although their bows were strong and their arrows swift, they did not reach even halfway to the six suns blazing in the heavens.

In great humility, then, the archers bowed low before the emperor and said: "However accurately we shoot at them, the suns will remain, for no arrow can reach them."

So Emperor Yao again sent forth his heralds and summoned Prince Ho-Yi of a neighboring tribe to the palace.

Once again the people thronged under the burning skies, for Prince Ho-Yi was a famous archer, and they wanted to see if his arrows could reach the suns. When everyone was assembled, Emperor Yao commanded: "Shoot down the six suns and save my people!"

Ho-Yi looked at the suns and he lifted his bow; but then he turned sadly to the emperor and said: "The six suns are just too far away for my slender arrows to reach them."

But at that very moment, Prince Ho-Yi saw the six bright suns reflected in a pool, and he thought: "Why wouldn't it be the same thing to shoot them there, where my arrows can reach?"

So he drew his great bow and the arrow flew and pierced the first sun, which disappeared at the bottom of the pool. He fired again, and the second sun disappeared, as well, into the water, then the third, the fourth, and the fifth suns.

When the sixth sun saw what was happening, he became so frightened that he quickly disappeared over the nearest hill. The ten village elders were quite content that the six suns had all been driven away, so the people returned, each to his own mud hut.

But when the villagers awakened from their long, deep sleep (for they were less worried now), there was no "next day," for the sixth sun was still fearful and he would not come out of the cave in which he was hiding and shine again on the earth. So the ten wise elders gathered once more in the dark to determine what could be done. They all agreed to find someone to summon the sixth sun from his hiding place, so that there could be a "next day."

First they brought a tiger, and he roared and roared at the sixth sun to come out; but the sixth sun only became very angry at this, since he didn't like the loud roaring. He replied: "I won't come out!"

Then the villagers brought a cow, thinking that her gentle lowing would surely lure the sun forth, but the sixth sun was still angry and sulking, and he said again: "I won't come out, and that's that!"

At last the people brought a fine fat cock to crow, and the sixth sun listened intently, and then he said: "My, what a lovely sound!" And he peeked out over the horizon to discover what could be making it.

As he peered down at them, the people all saw him, of course, and they cried out and shouted in gladness and joy. That was their welcome to the sun. And the sixth sun was so pleased at this that gradually he came out all the way; and then he fashioned a little red crown for the head of the fine fat cock!

And every morning early, since that faraway day, the cock wears his proud red crown when he crows to call forth the sun!

*   *   *

"How the Cock Got His Red Crown" is a tale from West China that was a favorite with itinerant storytellers. This is just one of various versions explaining how that red crown came to decorate the cock's jaunty head.

11 THE DOG

戊 狗

HSÜ   KOU

The Dog

In both Chinese and Japanese languages, the ideograph for "dog" is derived from the ancient pictogram for the animal. That pictogram was much admired by Confucius, so it is said.

The dog has lived a long time in China. Various breeds are shown in pictographic writings of the Shang Period (1766–1121 B.C.), in hunting scenes in the Ch'in tomb tiles (221–206 B.C.), in Han Dynasty bas-reliefs (206 B.C.–A.D. 220), in tomb figures of the T'ang Dynasty (A.D. 618–907), and in paintings from the beginning of the Sung Dynasty (A.D. 960), to the end of the Ch'ing Dynasty (A.D. 1912). As far back as Ch'in times, the Chinese boasted graceful hunting dogs or hounds. In the Han Period, greyhounds, chowchows, and Pekingese pugs were known.

The Buddhist (Cambodian) lion, a constantly recurring symbol in Chinese art and legend, is also allied with the dog; the lion, not native to Asia, and therefore known only through hearsay, was painted and carved as a mythical creature, with many of the characteristics of the dog. Indeed, the Pekingese pug was popularly referred to as the "lion dog," to associate it with the Buddhist "spirit lion." The nineteenth-century Empress Dowager Tzu Hsi declared that the Pekingese should be bred with a body like that of a hunting lion spying for its prey, and (so that it might be carried about in the sleeves of a robe) of "colors to suit costumes." Further, she decreed, if this precious pug should fall ill, one must "anoint it with the clarified fat of the leg of a snow-leopard, and give it to drink from throstle egg-shells full of the juice of custard-apples, in which are three pinches of shredded rhinoceros horn, and then apply piebald leeches; and, if it dies, remember that man is not immortal and thou must die too."

Some dogs became such great favorites of early emperors that they had official rank bestowed upon them, complete with appropriate costume! Such favored dogs were fed rare delicacies and protected by their own private guards.

Small wonder, then, that the possession of a dog in an Asian home came to indicate good fortune! More practically, a dog was valued for fidelity, and as both a guardian and a scavenger. Images of dogs for veneration came about because of the "Heavenly Dog Star," supposedly an unlucky star that devours the moon at the time of an eclipse. This same "Heavenly Dog Star" is also believed to be the soul of a young girl who died unmarried and continually seeks to snatch someone else's infant for her own. She desires to use the lost child as replacement so that she herself, the young girl, can be reincarnated as a mortal. Consequently she must be placated, and newborn infants are protected by a "dog's hair talisman," a ball made of a lock of the infant's own hair rolled up in some dog hair and sewed to the baby's clothing. For additional protection, children are sometimes given the name of an animal and provided with a silver dog collar, to induce the evil spirit to imagine that the child is really an animal and therefore not worth attention.

At the time of the moon's eclipse, temple gongs and bells are struck and firecrackers exploded to prevent the evil spirit of the Heavenly Dog Star from eating the lovely lunar orb.

The Japanese too pay great attention to the dog. They recognize two kinds of dog deities, called *inugami*: those employed in witchcraft, and those worshipped for protection. Mount Koya, south of Nara, where are found the central shrines of the Shingon sect of Buddhism, is believed to enjoy canine protection. It is said that the great Shingon leader, Kobo Daishi, while roaming over this mountain, met a Shinto god out hunting in the area, accompanied by two dogs, one white and one black. The god promised the saint protection for the Buddhist monastery in return for the building of a Shinto shrine. As a result of this happy exchange, dogs are perm'tted on Mount Koya, although all other animals are excluded.

A dog box called *inuhariko* is used by unsophisticated people as a talisman to protect a newborn child. Usually, two of these are given to a baby on the occasion of his *miyamairi*, the first visit to the shrine or temple for the naming ceremony. One box, surmounted by a male dog looking to the left, holds the baby's charms; the other, surmounted by a female dog looking to the right, contains toys and toilet articles. Later, such boxes can become the child's toys or amulets. If the child should suffer from a cold, holes are punched in the toy dog's nostrils to enable the child to breathe easier. If the child cannot sleep, the amulet is hung over his head.

There are numerous Japanese dog legends; one of the most popular is *Hakkenden*, or "The Story of the Eight Dogs," a tale adapted from the Chinese. It tells of the exploits of eight dog-headed heroes, the miraculous offspring of the Lady Fuse-hime, whose father forced her to marry the dog Yatsubara as a reward for the animal's having got rid of an enemy of the father who was besieging his province. The eight offspring of this marriage, with human bodies and heads of dogs, are considered to represent the Eight Cardinal Virtues.

Numerous stories are told of dogs saving their masters from harm or displaying extraordinary fidelity to their masters, even up to the moment of death. One classic tale of a faithful dog is that of Yorozu, a rebel, who, pursued by the imperial guard, fought heroically until, severely wounded and disastrously outnumbered, he performed the ritual *seppuku*. The court thereupon commanded that his body be cut into eight pieces and displayed publicly in the eight provinces of the realm. But, in the midst of a heavy storm (a classic sign of calamity), Yorozu's large white dog, looking first heavenward, then earthward, ran around his master's corpse, howling mournfully. Taking his master's head into his mouth, the dog dragged the body to an ancient burial mound, and then, lying down close to the body, the animal died in turn of self-imposed hunger. Hearing of this event, the court was moved to pity and commanded that a proper burial and tomb be provided both master and dog. This was done, and the sad event is commemorated in *netsuke* carvings of an emaciated dog with one paw resting on a skull.

Another such faithful dog was Hachiko, to whom a statue was erected in front of Tokyo's Shibuya Station. Every day for years, rain or shine or snow, Hachiko went to this station at a certain hour to greet his master on his return from work. But finally the master died. Unable to comprehend, Hachiko continued his daily trips to meet the train until he himself died of the burden of disappointment, grief, and age.

So people born in the Year of the Dog are expected to be possessed of many of these noble traits of their patron animal. They have a deep sense of duty and loyalty, they are extremely honest, and they get on well with others. Dog-year people inspire confidence and can safely be trusted with secrets. And they are strong champions of justice, taking up worthwhile causes, working doggedly at them, and seeing them through to success. They tend to be good at business affairs and are noted for their zeal in such matters. They usually remain cool under stress.

Their weaknesses are that they sometimes tend to be faultfinders and to have sharp tongues. At times they can be selfish, stubborn, and reveal rather eccentric behavior. They care very little for social life and often exhibit uneasiness in big gatherings of this nature.

Such people marry most successfully with representatives of the horse, tiger, or rabbit years.

Second choice for them would be someone from the years of the rat, snake, monkey, dog, or boar. Marriage with a person from the ox year or the Year of the Cock will not work out well. But the least successful marriage for someone from the dog year would be made with a mate from either the dragon or the ram year.

Kuro, the faithful dog

The morning star was shining with unusual brilliance in a serene and lovely autumn sky. Old Yasuke was making his way up Mount Shirahama, gun on shoulder, accompanied by his pet dog Kuro, who trotted along following the scent, sometimes running ahead, sometimes lagging behind. By the time they had achieved the half-way point on the mountain, morning had dawned completely. Kuro, a few yards ahead of his master, suddenly ran back to him, wagging his tail vigorously. He fastened his teeth in Yasuke's clothing, pulling him along to a spot where the hunter had set a snare. Peering down into it, Old Yasuke saw an animal tangled in the net and struggling for freedom. His heart beat with joy at the catch. The next moment his gun could be heard up and down the mountain. The animal fell limp and dead.

When he reached down and picked up his prize, Ya-suke saw that he had a plump fawn with a beautiful coat of fur. "This is a good start," said Yasuke to himself; and he set about skinning the animal then and there, as he anticipated the price that the fur would fetch. At that moment a loud bellowing of deer was heard from the summit of the mountain. Kuro pricked up his ears and stared hard in the direction of the noise, while his master, stopping his task, stood alert, with his gun at the level, ready to shoot at the first sight of game. For the moment there was in his mind only the thought of large fat deer with beautiful branched antlers. The dog, mad with excitement, started off ahead, dashing through heavy undergrowth as tall as he. In just a few minutes he was lost to sight. The bellowing above ceased, and Yasuke resumed his work.

The hunter was standing near a giant pine tree, hundreds of years old, one which the superstitious folk of nearby villages regarded with awe and reverence. They called it the "Home of the Tengu," the long-nosed goblin, and they believed that cutting off a single branch of that tree would mean certain death. His task completed, Yasuke started looking for his missing dog. The sun was now well up in the sky. Yasuke stood there for a long time, leaning on his gun. Still no sign of Kuro. Then, feeling intense fatigue, the hunter was about to sit down under the tree to rest when, with a furious barking, Kuro appeared from among the thick-grown reeds and ran up to him. Startled by some strange look of the dog, Yasuke stepped backward, crying out: "Stop barking, Kuro! Have you gone mad?" But the dog continued to bark, even more savagely. In a fit of real temper the hunter fetched his dog a hard blow with his fist, but this only caused the animal, totally frenzied, to howl with greater insistence.

Overcome finally by a sense of fatigue, Yasuke sat down under the tree, despite the dog's persistent disturbance. Kuro now started to snap indiscriminately at parts of his master's body, looking up from time to time at the top of the pine tree. This compelled Yasuke to jump to his feet in irritation, and when he noticed that both of his legs were bleeding, his reason became blinded with rage. To his eyes, Kuro no longer seemed a gentle and loving pet, a faithful companion, but rather a wild and ferocious wolf, thirsting for blood. Snatching his gun, leaning against the tree, Yasuke shot his dog, which fell at his feet in a pool of blood. Yasuke sat again at the foot of the pine tree to enjoy an undisturbed rest.

At that moment a small snake, about a foot long, dropped from the tree. Its eyes, immensely large and out of all proportion to its size, sparkled with a weird luster; its body was covered with square patterns. Yasuke had never before seen any snake like this. "Was it because of this little creature that Kuro barked so furiously?" he wondered. The snake continued to crawl toward him and was soon at his feet, licking at the toes of his right foot with its fiery tongue, a very large tongue (Yasuke thought) for so small a body.

Suddenly the eyes of the dead Kuro opened wide, and his body jerked a bit. And at the same moment the snake was thrown backward a little, as if by some invisible hand. But it returned at once to Yasuke's foot. Amused rather than alarmed by this seemingly innocent act of the little creature, Yasuke left it alone. But suddenly he became alarmed when he saw that the snake was beginning to swallow his toes one by one, until finally his whole foot, up to the ankle, was within the snake's jaw. Fear now got the better of curiosity, and the hunter shot at the snake's head. At that instant, Mount Shirahama rumbled with a deafening sound and was instantly enveloped in black clouds. The little snake was transformed into a monstrous serpent; when he looked at it, Yasuke fainted and fell to the ground. With one blood-curdling scream, the giant serpent started wriggling downhill, crushing under its tortuous body anything and everything that lay in its path, until finally it splashed into the sea at far-distant Kamiura. The black clouds, borne on the rising wind, followed closely on the path of the serpent, pouring down torrents of rain. Then they faded simultaneously with the vanishing of the monster into the sea.

Yasuke had an eleven-year-old son, Yaichi, who, together with his bedridden grandmother, took charge of the house while his father was away hunting. That morning, when they awakened, they heard the report of a gun in the direction of Mount Shirahama. This brought a smile to the old woman's face. Some time later another report was heard, this time accompanied by the familiar barking of Kuro. The old woman, beaming at the child, said: "We shall have a heavy bag today. Be quick, and go find your father so you can help him."

Yaichi started off at once. He was at the foot of the mountain, looking toward the summit, when he heard a third report of the gun, followed by a tremendous rumbling and shaking of the mountain. It knocked the boy senseless. When he came to himself some time later, he found himself surrounded by villagers who had hastened to the spot as soon as they heard the noises.

Prompted by anxiety for the father and son, the group ascended the mountain, and when they neared the pine tree, they were shocked to discover Yasuke lying unconscious and covered with blood, his gun still in his grasp. They tried to raise him to his feet, but he was immovable, as hard as a stone. Then, despite the absence of any wind, there was a series of rustling sounds in the tree. Everyone was totally at a loss to understand these mysteries.

Meantime Yasuke recovered consciousness and opened his eyes, crying out: "Oh, the snake! The snake! The dead body of Kuro. . . . " His voice trailed off and again he sank down senseless, with square patterns, exactly like those on the body of the snake he had shot, appearing over his entire body.

This gave the villagers a vague notion of how matters stood; and toward evening they carried the bodies of Yasuke and Kuro, both dead, down the mountainside and buried them, with proper rites, at the foot of the mountain.

*   *   *

"Kuro, the Faithful Dog" is one of a number of favorite Japanese tales about dogs faithful to their masters unto death. Some of these dogs are commemorated with statues.

 A dog named Fireball

Once upon a time, in the world above the skies, there was a land called the Land of Darkness. This was just one of many countries in that world, just as in our own universe we have many different nations.

As its name implies, this Land of Darkness had no light whatever. It was perpetually night in that country. Day in, day out, year in, year out, darkness reigned over the land.

The people of this country were quite accustomed to living without light. By listening carefully to differences in sound, and by feeling their way about, they were able to find what they wanted. The people had become, indeed, expert at groping about in the dark. To tell the truth, however, everybody was quite glum and unhappy. They were all so sick and tired of the ever-lasting blackness.

Their one cry was: "I wish we had some light! How wonderful it would be to have some light! I wish we could have both day and night, and not just night!"

Of course the king of the Land of Darkness also wanted light. "The world of man below has its sun and its moon," he reflected. "Isn't there, I wonder, some way of getting some light for us?" This thought ran continually through the king's mind.

Now it happened that in the Land of Darkness there were a great number of dogs. Everybody kept dogs. But among them all, one was really outstanding. He was a great shaggy creature, enormously strong and exceedingly clever.

This brave animal was endowed by nature with a gigantic mouth. Not only was his mouth exceptionally large, but it had the unique quality of being able to stand any amount of heat. This dog could actually carry the very hottest things in his mouth—even red-hot balls of fire. Of course in the Land of Darkness there were almost never any balls of fire, but even had there been a dozen a day, the dog could have carried them all. That is why the people of the Land of Darkness called him Fireball. For Fireball he truly was.

And that wasn't all. Fireball had four of the strongest and fastest legs in all the country. He could run hundreds and thousands of miles in the twinkling of an eye.

One day the king had an idea. "I do believe that dog could really run to the world of man, snatch away its sun, and fetch it back to our Land of Darkness." This was the king's thought.

The king then called together all the wise men of his kingdom, and told them of his bright new idea. They listened carefully, and when he had finished they all clapped their hands in approval and then praised their ruler highly for his wisdom.

"You are absolutely right, Your Highness" they said. "That's the only way to bring light to our country. Fireball will certainly succeed. You have really hit upon a wonderful idea."

Everyone was so overjoyed at the king's suggestion that they were completely carried away. They rejoiced, just as if Fireball had already brought the sun back in his mouth.

The king was happy too, to think that he had formulated such a fine plan. He ordered that preparations be made at once for Fireball's departure.

Fireball started out bravely on his long, long journey. It was a very lengthy trip indeed. Even with his strong, fast legs, it would take Fireball two years (at least) to reach the sun. But the dog never stopped to rest. He kept on running, day after day, month after month. And at last he reached the skies over the earth.

There it was, the bright sun shining in the sky! Soon the dog was right up to it. It was a huge round ball of fire. Fireball opened his enormous mouth and sank his teeth deeply into the sun, trying to tear it out of the sky. But it was hot—fearfully hot. It was certainly many times hotter than any fireball he had ever carried in his mouth before! The animal succeeded in getting the sun in his mouth, but then he simply could not endure the heat. He felt as if his whole body were melting away from the heat of the sun.

"It's no use. The sun is just too hot. At this rate, I won't ever be able to tear the sun out of the sky," said the poor dog to himself. So he gave up, and spat the sun out of his mouth. Then, filled with chagrin, he returned to the Land of Darkness.

When the king saw Fireball come back without the sun, he was very, very disappointed. Then he thought: "If the sun is too hot for this animal, then why not at least have him bring back the moon? That would at least give us some light."

So he commanded Fireball: "Go to the moon and bring it back! It should not be nearly so hot as the sun." Thus, even before Fireball was able to rest from his long journey to the sun, he was ordered off to the moon.

After a long journey, Fireball again reached the skies over the world of man. There, hanging from the sky like a bright lantern, was the moon. It shone with a blue-white light. And, sure enough, it did not give off any heat.

"This time I shall be able to take back some light," thought Fireball.

So he put his big mouth to the moon and took one bite, just as he had tried to do with the sun. But oh, it was certainly very, very cold! In fact it was freezing cold, just like a huge lump of ice. Fireball did succeed in getting all the moon into his mouth. But he just could not bear the cold. It seemed as if his whole body would freeze. So once again he was forced to give up his project. He spat out the moon and returned in total despondency to the Land of Darkness.

When the king saw Fireball come back without the moon, he was again very disappointed. But his wish to help give light to his country remained unaltered. In fact, the more the king thought about the sun and the moon and how difficult it was to get either one, the more he craved having one or the other of them brought back. Once more he summoned Fireball to him, ordering him to go forth again and get the sun.

Tired as he was, Fireball again set bravely forth. But yet again he failed in his purpose. He did succeed in getting the sun into his mouth, but, just as before, he could not withstand that terrible heat. Once more then, Fireball came back empty-mouthed.

The king, sorely disappointed, next ordered Fireball to try for the moon again. But it was the same story. When he got the moon into his mouth, it was as cold as ever. He simply could not stand it—that was how cold the moon was.

Five times, ten times, twenty times, over and over and over again, Fireball repeated the same hopeless journey. And each time he failed. And as many times as the dog failed, just as many times did the king strengthen his resolve to bring light to his land.

But the sun was just too hot, and the moon just too cold. No matter how brave and strong and willing Fireball was, this one feat he could not accomplish.

Still the king of the Land of Darkness would not give up. His obsession to get light for his country, his kingdom, had now become an overwhelming passion, deeply rooted in his mind. He was sure that, no matter if Fireball failed a hundred times, nay, a thousand, ten thousand times, there would come finally a day when this wonder dog would prevail.

"Just watch," the king told himself. "One of these days Fireball will come home in triumph with either the sun or the moon."

So Fireball continued to go to the sun and the moon by turns. Many, many years passed. Fireball was no longer a young dog. He was no longer so strong and fleet as once he had been. But the king of the Land of Darkness kept on ordering the dog to go in pursuit of the sun and the moon.

Even to this present day, Fireball continues his distant trips to the skies above the world of man, first to the sun and then to the moon.

The eclipses of the sun and the moon are signs that Fireball, the brave and loyal dog from the Land of Darkness, is still living, still trying to carry out the command of his king. Each time that he grabs the sun or the moon in his mouth, he is making another valiant attempt to bring light back to his king.

And, never doubt it for a moment, Fireball will go right on trying again and again, through eternity. That's the kind of faithful dog he is.

*   *   *

"A Dog Named Fireball," surely one of the most delightful explanations ever made of natural phenomena, comes from Korea.

The dog stone

In the village of Asahi in Bizen Prefecture, there is a famous stone known as *Inu Ishi,* or Dog Stone. This stone is popularly reverenced as a deity. It is said that once a stonemason who attempted to cut it was sent flying into the air and killed outright. Here is the legend connected with that miraculous stone.

About eleven hundred years ago, the Imperial Minister of the Left, a man named Sugawara Michizane, started off on a pilgrimage to the Kumano Shrine. But by the time he reached the ferry over the river Kinokawa (in the Prefecture of Kii), he had spent all his travel funds and was unable to pay the toll. Then he recalled that his dog, who was accompanying him, had the amazing power of producing gold from his body. So he offered the dog to the ferryman, saying: "I am so sorry that I have no money at all left to pay you for ferrying me; but this dog of mine will bring you one piece of gold in return for one bowl of sand given it for food each day. So please keep this dog and this bowl till I come again in the future to pay you the money I owe. Just one word of caution: do not ever overfeed this animal!"

More than satisfied with this really extraordinary method of payment, the boatman carried Michizane across the river.

Sure enough, the dog brought the ferryman one piece of gold every day in return for one bowl of sand, as regularly as a clock; and thus, to the great surprise and bewilderment of his fellow villagers, the ferryman soon became a rich man. But, like most humans, the more he got, the more he wanted, until one day he said to himself: "If the amount of sand is doubled, the amount of gold should surely be doubled accordingly." And so, in spite of Michizane's warning, he gave the dog two bowls of sand in place of one. Contrary to his expectations, however, this brought him not one single coin, to say nothing of gold. What was worse, the dog came down with convulsions and died in the middle of the night. Vexed at the result of his own indiscretion, the ferryman threw the body of the dead dog into the river Kinokawa.

Some years later, Michizane, falling victim to a plot of the Minister of the Right, was condemned to banishment to Dazaifu in Kyushu. On his way there, he was sailing off the coast near Kawaguchi in the Province of Bizen. Night had fallen, the sky had clouded over, the tide was running strong, and Michizane's boat was in danger of being sucked into a whirlpool. Just at that moment, however, Michizane heard the sound of a dog barking, as if from the shore, and, listening carefully, he felt sure that it was the barking of his own dog, the one he had left with the ferryman. At once Michizane ordered the boatman to steer his course in that direction; thus, snatched from the jaws of death by having so changed their course, Michizane and his crew were able to reach the shore in safety. But what Michizane found there was not the dog he expected, just a large stone in the shape of a dog.

Michizane stayed overnight beside the stone; then, before departing on the next day, he planted a number of young pine trees in commemoration of the incident.

Even today, those pines remain as fresh and as green as ever, even though all the other plants and trees in that area have perished as the result of noxious smoke from a nearby smelting plant.

And, for some unexplained reason, the bark of those particular pine trees is credited with power to alleviate toothache!

*   *   *

"The Dog Stone" is an old Japanese story, and is told here as adapted from Richard Dorson's version.

12 THE BOAR

亥 猪

HAI　CHU

The Boar

 The wild boar has played a prominent role in the mythologies of many primitive peoples. Usually it fulfills the role of benefactor, supplying man with food as well as with the pleasures of the chase, and delivering man from one of his most dangerous enemies, the snake. In any encounter between the wild boar and the snake, the snake can avert defeat only by making a fast getaway.

Among Semitic peoples, the pig was considered sacred because he taught man the art of ploughing through turning up the soil with his snout. In Mesopotamia, the divine mother was called the Earth Sow, the symbol of creative energy. The boar played an important role in festivals of the vernal equinox, and the god personifying the summer sun was believed to be slain annually by a wild boar. In Germanic folklore, the boar was associated with the storm and, as a fertility symbol, with the harvest.

In the most ancient Asian drawings, the wild boar is shown holding the earth on its powerful tusks. In this form it was believed to represent a cosmic creation legend of primitive peoples. So, as one of the Zodiac signs of early India and China, its use dates back to remote times.

In India the boar was first known as the avatar or incarnation of Brahma, the Creator and the first person of the Hindu trinity, who, as Prajapati (in the form of a boar) rescued the earth from the waters of oblivion. (It is said that this particular boar issued from the god's nostrils as a creature about the size of a thumb, then immediately grew to the size of an elephant.) Later on, the creation was attributed to Vishnu, the Preserver and the second god in the Hindu triad; Vishnu infused a part of his divine essence into the form of a wild boar, dove into an abyss of chaotic water, and, after a struggle of a thousand years, slew the great demon Hiranyaksha and rescued the earth from demonic control.

The great Hindu epic, the *Ramayana*, gives an account of this creation myth, crediting Brahma with taking the form of a boar that raised up the earth and created the whole world. " . . . the mighty boar, whose eyes were like the lotus, whose body was vast as the Nila mountains, and of the dark colors of the lotus leaves, uplifted upon his ample tusks the earth from its lowest regions. . . . " Tradition claims that this mammoth boar was forty-five miles in breadth and five thousand miles tall, that his color was that of a dark cloud, and that his roar was like thunder. His bulk was vast as a mountain; his tusks were white, sharp, and fearful. Fire flashed from his eyes like lightning, and he was radiant like the sun. His shoulders were round, flat, and large; he strode along like a powerful lion. His haunches were fat, his loins slender, and his body altogether smooth and beautiful.

This boar, known as Varahi, the third incarnation

of Vishnu, was worshipped as a feminine deity—as the queen of heaven, the metamorphosis of the sun, the source of all life, who mated with the primeval, productive pig. In Tibet this boar is known as the Adamantine Sow or the Diamond Sow, who became incarnate in the abbess of a convent at Yamdok Lake. There was an ancient tradition that there had once been an abbess with a growth resembling a pig's head behind one of her ears. A Mongol warrior named Yun Gar attacked the cloister and challenged the abbess to emerge and reveal her sow's head. When she failed to do so, he forced his way into the building, but found it surprisingly unoccupied except for a number of pigs, one of them much larger than the others. So startled was the attacker that he refrained from pillaging the premises. Thereupon the pigs were transformed into monks and nuns, the large sow becoming the abbess herself. Not surprisingly, Yun Gar was so impressed by this miracle that he was converted to Buddhism on the spot and endowed the monastery generously. This legend is reminiscent of Homer's Circe, who transformed the companions of Ulysses into pigs but was later compelled to return them to human form.

The wild boar is native to both China and Japan, where he is commonly called "mountain pig" or "mountain whale." In classical Chinese language, however, the name means "long-snout military officer," or "the long-nosed general," because his reckless courage and his savage, ferocious nature make him a symbol for the human fighter. Many ancient legends, in fact, suggest that some great warrior is in actuality a reincarnated boar.

As one example of this, the *Yi Chien Chih* tells of a famous Sung-dynasty general, Yeh Fei, who spent his formative years in the company of a Buddhist priest. The priest recognized in the boy the spirit of a boar, and as a result he was able to foretell both the young man's future career and his premature death, which he attributed to jealousy on the part of a premier. All that he said came eventually to pass, and, following Yeh Fei's death, the guilty premier had a troublesome dream in which he was attacked by a man with a boar's head. So realistic was this event that the premier was unable to get over it, and he soon died.

Another ancient Chinese legend tells of a different premier who, out hunting, killed a huge wild boar, cooked it, and ate it. That night he was visited in a dream by a large man who thanked him for having released his spirit from that boar, who had held it. Now, he declared, he could be reborn as a human, and a great warrior. The following day one of the premier's concubines gave birth to a son who in later years became one of China's foremost generals.

In the *Hsi Yu Chi* ("Journey to the Western Paradise"), Hsu Hsuan-chuang, or T'ang Seng, the pilgrim monk who made the journey to the West in order to procure the Buddhist scriptures for the emperor of China (the work is a dramatization of the entrance of Buddhism into China from India), was accompanied by a monkey spirit, Sun Hou-tzu, and by a pig spirit, Chu Pa-chieh. This pilgrim priest symbolized human conscience, which measures all its actions; the monkey spirit represented human nature, which is prone to all evil; and the pig spirit, represented as carrying a muckrake, symbolized the coarser passions, which are constantly at war with conscience. The pig was called the Chief Divine Altar Cleanser.

In the Chinese language, the character *chia*, meaning "family" or "home," is made up of a pig under a roof.

In Japanese history, as well as legend, the wild boar has been extensively noted. And he is noted as well in Japanese art. The animal is first noted in the *Kojiki* (A.D. 712). Because Japan has traditionally exalted the warrior, it is not surprising that the boar should be idealized for its fighting qualities. In fable, the God of War is sometimes shown riding on the back of a boar. To the Japanese, this animal symbolizes courage and steadfastness, because of the way he charges his enemy directly, never flinching, never turning to run away, but instead striking out determinedly, meeting the antagonist head on, and holding to a fixed position. (In honesty it must be mentioned that some people feel they sense the opposite characteristics in the boar; they view him as a wild and foolish beast who plunges ahead senselessly, attacking everything in his path, even when there is no provocation. So they have a saying: "as crazy as a wild hog.")

But many Japanese women celebrate the Day of the Boar by offering glutinous rice cakes called *o-mochi* to their patron saints, praying that they may be favored, like the wild boar, with many offspring, all of them possessed of that animal's total courage.

Another countryside tradition involves an October festival celebrating the young of the wild boar with special rice cakes offered at family altars. It is further believed that if anyone eats *o-mochi* pounded at the hour of the wild boar (9–11 p.m.) on the day of the boar, he will be free of all sicknesses.

Japanese painters are fond of showing the wild boar as the steed of the *tengu* king Sojobo, and as the companion of the famous Kintaro, or Golden Boy. In the eighteenth century the famous painter Maruyama Okyo saw a wild boar lying on the ground in the forest and made a painting of him. One of his friends, a hunter, remarked that it was not a good painting because it failed somehow to reveal the animal's latent power. The next day Okyo returned to the forest, and, to his surprise, saw the boar lying still in the same spot. He was not sleeping, as he had supposed. The boar was dead. So it turned out that Okyo's painting, if not true to life, was true to death!

The boar appears repeatedly in Japanese legend. In the story of the Hare of Inaba, when the Princess of Yakami chose Onamuchi over the eighty brothers, those brothers tried to trick the favored man by telling him that they would drive a red boar down the mountain Tema and that he must catch him or be slain by them. Then they kindled a great fire, heated a huge stone in the shape of a boar, and rolled it down the mountainside; when the unfortunate Onamuchi caught it, he was so badly burned that he perished. (His grieving mother later had him restored to life through the intercession of the gods.)

Another boar legend tells of Prince Yamatodake, who once encountered a mountain god in the shape of a boar as big as a bull. The prince exclaimed: "I can vanquish the god of this mountain without any weapons!" He then ascended the mountain and on its slope met another white boar. The prince said: "I haven't time to kill you now, but I will take care of you on my way down." Then he continued to the top of the mountain. But the mountain god caused a heavy ice storm to descend, so confusing the prince that he lost his direction and failed to carry out his plan.

Legend also relates the tale of another prince, Kagosaka, who conspired against his empress but died soon thereafter of the bite of a wild boar. His followers considered this a bad omen for their enterprise and so they abandoned it.

In the fifth century A.D., the Emperor Yuryaku is said to have also run afoul of a wild boar. He was ascending the mountain Katsuraga when a boar came rushing at him. Although the ruler wounded the boar with a speedy arrow, the animal continued to charge him. The prudent emperor wisely climbed a nearby elder tree, finding refuge in the nick of time. Safely settled on a stout branch, he at once composed a poem about the occasion.

In 1193, when the great warrior Yoritomo gave a hunting party at the foot of Mount Fuji, a boar suddenly broke cover and, wounded and maddened, headed straight at the hunters, too fast to be hit with their arrows. In an instant the warrior Nitan-no-Shiro Yadatsune sprang from Yoritomo's bodyguard and, casting aside his bow and arrows, and leaping on his horse, he made straight for the boar, which turned to attack him. Like a flash, Nitan leaped on the back of the beast, with his own back to the animal's head. Grasping the tail, Nitan clung to the speeding animal until he found a chance to draw his dagger and stab him to death. Thereupon, so it is said, he received an ovation "so great as to shake the surrounding hills."

A favorite Japanese legend tells of a monkey and a boar, servants to a rich farmer, who were great friends. One day the boar overheard their master say: "I believe I shall kill that monkey. He is really a good-for-nothing fellow and only frightens the children with his antics." The boar relayed this information to his friend, and together they pondered what to do. Finally they evolved a plan. The boar would kidnap the child; the monkey would run after him, snatch the child back from him, and return it to the farmer, who was bound to feel grateful. So they did just this, and their ruse proved successful. The monkey's life was spared and the farmer, to show his deep appreciation, provided him with a totally pampered existence. Ah, but what happened to the boar at the hands of the farmer? That is not known. Perhaps the farmer killed the poor animal, since boar's meat was thought to be efficacious against baldness and epilepsy!

At the annual festival of Futara Mountain, a boar dance is still performed annually to commemorate the act of Prince Jigaku: his sermons against the taking of any life caused two brothers, Banji and Banzaburo, to give up hunting and help establish the Nikkō mountain area as a bird and animal sanctuary. It is said that, of all the animals, the wild boar felt particularly grateful for this act and went to Priest Jigaku to express his thanks. But the priest sent him off to thank Banji instead.

Many Japanese shrines are held sacred to special *kami*, or spirit messengers. The Atago Shrine is dedicated to the spirit of the boar.

Because of its value, the wild boar symbolizes, quite practically, the wealth of the forest. He always maintains his lair in wooded hill country; and in modern times he is usually snared in deep pits dug at the foot of a mountain and covered with deep grass for concealment. The bristles growing along his back have always been an important export and a good source of foreign exchange for the Chinese.

As might be expected, people born in the Year of the Boar are thought to be courageous and headstrong. They possess tremendous fortitude and great inner strength. It is difficult to deter or deflect them, once they have set a course of action. Sometimes this attitude makes them reckless, and, as a result, they come to grief, afterwards expressing deep regret for their action. So they must be warned to think before acting.

Because they are impulsive, boar year people can be victimized by the unscrupulous. In general, however, they are honest, gallant, chivalrous, pure, and persistent. Although short-tempered, they really dislike quarreling, and try hard to avoid the necessity for it. Basically, they are kind and affectionate individuals who, once they make friends, usually retain them for life.

Such people are well informed and rather studious though not necessarily profound thinkers. They tend not to say much, as a rule; but if they do open up, they will talk things out frankly, even though they are basically shy. This shyness leads them to try to solve their own problems, rather than turning to outsiders for aid.

Rabbit- and ram-year people make the best marriage partners for those born in the Year of the Boar. Their second-best choice would be someone from the rat, ox, tiger, dragon, horse, cock, or dog years. A wedding with someone from the monkey or boar years is to be shunned. But the least successful marriage of all for someone of the boar year would be made with a person from the Year of the Snake.

The tower that reached from earth to heaven

Far away, on the western borders of Tibet, there is a country called the Land of Sekkim. In the Land of Sekkim lives a race of men called Lepchas. And in the race of men called Lepchas there was a farmer named Wu who had many little pigs.

One day, when the winds blew strong from the mountains of Tibet, Farmer Wu's little pigs all ran away. Now Farmer Wu loved his little pigs more than anything else in the world, so he wrapped a turban about his head and went out to look for them. He climbed steep mountain passes and then he ran down into valleys. For many days and weeks he wandered on, always calling to his little lost pigs. He wandered so far that one day, to his great surprise, he found himself in heaven!

Now Farmer Wu had often wondered whether the country called heaven was at all like the country called Sekkim; great was his delight, therefore, to see lovely rolling hills and many little pigs running about. He was sure that some of them must be his own little pigs that had run away. He was so happy that he begged to stay there forever and ever. But the people in heaven replied:

"Oh no, you are not yet ready to stay in heaven. You must go back to earth for a few years more."

The way seemed very long to Farmer Wu as he trudged back to earth. But when he reached the Land of Sekkim, he told the men called Lepchas all about the country called heaven, with many little pigs running about. The men called Lepchas were so excited that they all decided they would build themselves a tower to reach to heaven.

"With a tower to reach to heaven, we can climb up there from our own country, without taking the long journey over the steep mountain passes."

Every man in the Land of Sekkim went to work on the tower. One storey on top of another storey, up and up they built it, one storey atop another. As they worked on, they looked up and saw that they were getting nearer and nearer to heaven.

As each storey was completed, they left one little man of Sekkim there to act as guard.

So they worked on for many days and many months. Finally, after two long years, their tower needed only one more storey to touch the country called heaven. Then the little men of Sekkim grew impatient.

"If only we had some big hooks, we could pull ourselves up into heaven without building the last storey," they said to one another.

This was a fine idea. So the man at the top called to the man on the storey below him: "Send us hooks!"

And he called to the man below him: "Send us hooks!"

And he in turn called to the man below: "Send us hooks!"

And *he* called out to the man below: "Send us hooks!"

And so on, from storey to storey, the call made its way down to the Land of Sekkim. But on the way, a very sad thing happened. The message was repeated so many, many times that it got twisted and, when it finally reached the bottom, instead of being still "Send us hooks!" it had become "Cut us down!"

Whereupon the men called Lepchas got out their great stone axes and cut down the tower that reached almost to heaven. It crashed in a heap on the ground.

And to this very day, far away on the western border of Tibet, there can be seen a flat green spot deep in a valley, right in the heart of a thick jungle forest. And, as they pass that spot, the people say: "Do you see that spot in the deep valley? That is the place where the Tower of Sekkim fell down—the Tower of Sekkim that almost reached the country called heaven, where the trees are green and rolling, and many little pigs run about."

* * *

"The Tower That Reached from Earth to Heaven" is a tale from Tibet.

The priest and the boar

Near Mount Atago, in Yamashiro Province, there once lived a huntsman named Tarobei. He was a hardy and plucky fellow of an adventurous turn of mind. One day he paid a visit to a priest, chief of a Buddhist temple which stood not far from where he lived. The priest, who had apparently been longing for somebody's companionship, just to chat, welcomed the visit with joy and cordiality, and entertained his guest with interesting stories. Suddenly, then, he lowered his voice, and bringing his lips close to Tarobei's ear, he whispered:

"I have something to tell you about the great blessing which I am enjoying through Buddha's grace."

"What is that? Pray tell me all about it," the huntsman responded, also in a hushed voice.

"I have been reciting the sutras for many years, and finally Buddha, in recognition of my sincerity, has sent me a Fugen Bosatsu, who comes to meet me every night on the back of a white elephant. But you must promise not to breathe a word about this to anybody."

"All right, Reverend Sir, I promise. But is it truly possible that such a thing can be?"

"Yes, there cannot be the slightest doubt about it. If you feel inclined to doubt it, stay here with me until nightfall, and then, I promise you, you will be convinced of the truth of what I say."

Tarobei assented to the priest's proposal and remained that full day at the temple.

Evening came. The priest and the huntsman took baths, purified themselves, and waited for the appearance of the Fugen Bosatsu. Hour after hour passed, until it was midnight. Then, all of a sudden, the top of the hill brightened, as if the moon were about to appear, and the watchers felt as if a celestial breeze had floated into their room. Suddenly they saw before them Fugen Bosatsu riding on the back of a pure white elephant.

The priest bowed to the august figure again and again, and shed tears of joy and gratitude.

"My dear Tarobei! Do you see him? How thankful we should feel for this marvelous condescension!"

"Yes, I do see him, indeed. And I don't know how to express my thanks to Bosatsu-sama for his great trouble in coming such a distance." While responding thus, the huntsman bowed in reverence to the saint. But within himself, while he was praying, he was saying:

"It is truly a marvel that his sacred body can be seen by such a man as I, who have committed so many sins against the teachings of the Buddha, by killing beasts and birds. I fear that some fox may be playing us a trick. I think I will test to see if this is really a genuine Bosatsu or not. If it is true, then I will surrender my hunter's life, shave my head, take the robe, and become a priest myself."

So the hunter took up his bow, which he had secretly brought along with him, and shot at the breast of Bosatsu-sama. There was a mournful cry, then no trace of either Bosatsu or the white elephant to be seen.

The astonished priest flew into a rage and exclaimed:

"You disgraceful, treacherous man! How dare you commit an audacious and totally unprovoked crime like this?"

Tarobei replied in a calm and passionless voice:
"You need not make such a great fuss about my conduct. I doubted in my heart that this was the real Bosatsu, as you claimed. So I tried to find out the truth about it, that's all. If anyone is to be punished, it must be I, not you. So put yourself at ease on that score."

But the priest would not listen to the huntsman's logic; he cursed and lamented his visitor's outrage all through the night.

In the morning, the two men went together to the spot where the white elephant seemed to have been standing the preceding evening. There they found the ground stained with blood. In the woods, about one meter from the spot, they spied the body of a huge white boar with the huntsman's arrow in his breast.

* * *

"The Priest and the Boar" is a Japanese tale which is told in many versions.

The pig that was too clever

Once upon a time, long ago, there lived in Tsan-yang village a certain Mr. Li. Everyone called him Li Tai-yeh, or "Big Master" Li, because he was the wealthiest man around. His farm was huge—three hundred *mou*, at least—and his house had one hundred rooms and a spacious courtyard. No one was the least bit jealous of him, because Li Tai-yeh, unlike many rich people, was very generous with his wealth. His love for animals was well known in the district, and indeed the animals also reciprocated that love. Eventually Li Tai-yeh came to have a good number of animals of various kinds on his farm. Some of them he acquired in the marketplace, but most of them wandered into his farmyard from the countryside around and just stayed on, because Farmer Li fed them well, yet demanded nothing from them in return.

Yet these animals instinctively wanted to help their benefactor in whatever way they could. So Hei-erh (the black dog) was the watchman. He saw to it that no strangers passed through the master's compound without being challenged.

The big rooster, who was called Chi-erh, always awakened the workers in the morning, calling out in a very loud voice, rain or shine, whenever the first light of dawn streaked the horizon: "Get up and go to work! Get up and work!"

The yellow striped tomcat, called Hu-erh, or Little Tiger, was an independent soul, roaming around wherever and whenever he pleased; but at night he was always on sentry duty to keep the rats from entering the house or barn.

The horse took on the drawing of the farmer's cart as his special task, and the water buffalo pulled the plough through the rice paddies. The donkey carried the Young Master, Li Tai-yeh's son, to school on his back. So, even though the Big Master asked nothing, everybody carried out some duty willingly and happily.

All, that is, except the pig.

This pig was a smart fellow called Chu Lao-erh. He thought about everything he saw going on, and he reasoned to himself: "Since everyone else is working except me, but Big Master is willing to go on feeding me, why should I work? He doesn't ask me to do anything at all. The food is free, all I want—why shouldn't I just take it easy, eat as much as I like, and rest?"

So Chu Lao-erh ate heavily, and then, when his meal was ended, he lay down in the muddy pond and got himself so filthy all over that the other animals preferred not to come near him. He slept until noon every day, waking up just in time to eat an enormous lunch; then he took a long and lovely siesta that lasted until dinnertime. After a huge, heavy dinner, he returned to bed and slept soundly through the night.

Occasionally another animal would waken him and suggest: "Why not do some useful work yourself, and get some exercise in order to reduce?" But Chu Lao-erh always pretended to be stupid and not to understand. He refused to answer any questions. He just grunted, rolled over on his other side, and slept again.

As a result of this regime, Chu Lao-erh became fatter and fatter and always felt that he was too tired to work anyway! He had caught himself in a vicious circle. Sometimes he even felt too tired to eat, and he took to complaining about the quality of the food he was served. He grunted that his meals were not properly prepared. Well, as everyone knows, complainers usually get results. So everyone at the farm began to think that the pig was really not feeling very well, and they took pains to feed him more and better food than anyone else got. Before long, Chu Lao-erh was the hugest pig that had ever been seen anyplace!

Meantime, Li Tai-yeh's neighbor, a man called Chiang-san, visited the farm and saw this fat pig. He said to Li Tai-yeh: "This Chu Lao-erh does nothing for you at all. I'd be willing to exchange my ducks for him. They will at least lay eggs for you."

Li Tai-yeh saw nothing wrong with this reasoning, and so he agreed to the proposition and let Chang-san drag the reluctant pig away. Chu Lao-erh was deeply unhappy because he knew that the Chiang family was poor and their farm would never be as good an eating place for him as Big Master's had been. He screamed and grunted and squealed so loud and so constantly that Chiang-san eventually called in help to tie him up by his four legs. Then he slid a shoulder pole in between the legs, hoisted him up (with some assistance) and carried him away to the market. That was the end of Chu Lao-erh. No one ever saw him again!

Ancient wisdom tells us that wise men often appear deliberately to be foolish or stupid; but that if a smart man appears to be a fool, he may just outsmart himself through his own foolishness. Two ancient sayings illustrate this point: "*Ta chih ro yu*," which means, "Great wisdom appears at times to be foolish as well"; and "*Tsung-ming pei tsung-ming wu*," or, "Smart people often defeat themselves by their own cleverness!"

And that is probably what happened in the case of Chu Lao-erh!

*   *   *

"The Pig That Was Too Clever" comes from the Chinese classics.

BIBLIOGRAPHY

Ball, Katherine M. *Decorative Motifs of Oriental Art.* New York: Dodd Mead & Co., 1927.

Blyth, R. H. *Oriental Humor.* Tokyo: Hokuseido Press, 1959.

Chiba, Reiko. *The Japanese Fortune Calendar.* Rutland, Vermont, and Tokyo: Charles E. Tuttle Co., Inc., 1967.

Chavannes, Edouard. "Le cycle Turc des douze animaux." *T'oung Pao,* series 2, vol. 7. Paris, 1897.

Christie, Anthony. *Chinese Mythology.* Middlesex, England: Hamlin Publishing Group, Ltd., 1968.

de Bary, William Theodore: Wing-Tsit Chan; and Watson, Burton, eds. *Sources of Chinese Tradition.* New York: Columbia University Press, 1960.

Dorson, Richard M. *Folk Legends of Japan.* Rutland, Vermont, and Tokyo: Charles E. Tuttle Co., Inc., 1962.

Eberhard, Wolfram, trans. *Chinese Fairy Tales and Folk Tales.* London: Kegan Paul, Trench, Trubner & Co., Ltd., 1937.

Hume, Lotta Carswell. *Favorite Children's Stories from China and Tibet.* Rutland, Vermont, and Tokyo: Charles E. Tuttle Co., Inc., 1962.

Joya, Mock. *Things Japanese.* Tokyo: Tokyo News Service, Ltd., 1960.

Kim So-un. *The Story Bag: A Collection of Korean Folktales.* Translated by Setsu Higashi. Rutland, Vermont, and Tokyo: Charles E. Tuttle Co., Inc., 1955.

Lin Yu-tang. *Famous Chinese Short Stories.* New York: The John Day Co., 1952.

Lum, Peter. *Fabulous Beasts*. New York: Pantheon Books, 1951.

Mackenzie, Donald A. *Myths of China and Japan*. London: The Gresham Publishing Co., Ltd., n.d.

Sakade, Florence, ed. *Japanese Children's Stories*. Rutland, Vermont, and Tokyo: Charles E. Tuttle Co., Inc., 1959.

Sun, Ruth Q. *Land of Seagull and Fox: Folk Tales of Vietnam*. Tokyo: John Weatherhill Co., Inc., 1966.

Volker, T. *The Animal in Far Eastern Art*. Leiden: E. J. Brill, 1950.

Werner, E. T. C. *A Dictionary of Chinese Mythology*. New York: The Julian Press, Inc., 1961.

_____. *Myths and Legends of China*. London: George C. Harrap & Co., Ltd., 1958.

White, Beatrice. "Medieval Animal Lore," *Anglia* 72 (1958).

Williams, C. A. S. *Encyclopedia of Chinese Symbolism and Art Motives*. New York: The Julian Press, Inc., 1960. (Originally published by Kelly & Walsh, Shanghai.)

Yang Hsien-yi and Yang, Gladys, trans. *Ancient Chinese Fables*. Peking: Foreign Languages Press, 1957.

Zong In-Sob. *Folk Tales from Korea*. London: Routledge & Kegan Paul, Ltd., 1952.

Yetts, W. P. *Symbolism in Chinese Art*. Leiden: E. J. Brill, 1912.

Other Titles in the Tuttle Library

JAPANESE HAIKU: Its Essential Nature, History, and Posibilities in English, with Selected Examples *by Kenneth Yasuda*

JAPANESE TALES OF MYSTERY AND IMAGINATION *by Edogawa Rampo, translated by James B. Harris*

THE JOURNEY *by Jiro Osaragi, translated by Ivan Morris*

KAPPA: A Satire *by Ryunosuke Akutagawa, translated by Geoffrey Bownas*

KWAIDAN: Stories and Studies of Strange Things *by Lafcadio Hearn*

A LATE CHRYSANTHEMUM: Twenty-one Stories from the Japanese *by Fumiko Hayashi and others, selected and translated by Lane Dunlop*

THE LIFE OF AN AMOROUS MAN *by Saikaku Ihara, translated by Kengi Hamada*

MODERN JAPANESE STORIES: An Anthology *edited by Ivan Morris, translated by Edward Seidensticker, George Saito, Geoffry Sargent, and Ivan Morris*

MONKEY'S RAINCOAT: Linked Poetry of the Basho School with Haiku Selections *translated by Leonore Mayhew*

A NET OF FIREFLIES: Japanese Haiku and Haiku Paintings *translated by Harold Stewart*

PAGODA, SKULL, AND SAMURAI: 3 Stories by Rohan Koda *translated by Chieko Irie Mulhern*

THE PAPER DOOR AND OTHER STORIES *by Shiga Naoya, translated by Lane Dunlop*

THE PORNOGRAPHERS *by Akiyuki Nozaka, translated by Michael Gallagher*